COASTAL NEW ENGLAND
WINTERFARE AND HOLIDAY
COOKING

By
Sherri Eldridge

Thanks for a
great stay !!
Peter & Marion
Martinez

Illustrations by
Robert Groves
Nadine Pranckunas

The gratitude of the author is extended to the Maine Chapter of the American Heart Association for the guidance and information provided. The use of the Association's name to convey the goals of this series of books is also gratefully appreciated. For each book sold, the publisher will make a contribution to further the life-preserving efforts of the American Heart Association.

For additional copies of:

Coastal New England Winterfare & Holiday Cooking
Coastal New England Summertime Cooking
Coastal New England Fall Harvest Cooking
Coastal New England Spring Cooking

use the order form in the back of the book or send $11.95 per book (Maine residents add state sales tax), plus shipping of $2.00 for the first book and $1.00 for each additional book to the publisher:

Coastal New England Publications
P.O. Box 55
Salisbury Cove, Maine 04672

VISA and Master Card are accepted. Credit card orders may call (207) 288-8988.

Coastal New England Cookbooks may be obtained by retail stores, or organizations for fund- raising projects, at special rates. Contact the publisher at the above address or phone number.

© 1995 Sherri A. Eldridge

ISBN: 1-886862-01-X (Winterfare & Holiday Cooking)
ISBN: 1-886862-04-4 (4 Volume Set)

First printing: March 1995
Second printing: June 1995 (Revised)

PRINTED IN THE U.S.A.

50%
TOTAL RECOVERED FIBER
15% POST-CONSUMER FIBER

FORWARD

On a cold winter day, hearty recipes created in Coastal New England towns warm households across the nation. Just as the harsh coastal climate brought together the people who made New England their home, the recipes developed by the settlers were shared at sewing bees and socials. Today, we share food and celebration at potluck suppers, in the company of friends and relatives. As New England has become more culturally diverse with every new generation, each has added an interpretation of flavor to expand the coastal New England cuisine.

We are benefited today by a wealth of nutritional knowledge, which has tremendously increased our expectancy to live a long and productive life. The American Heart Association has developed sound guidelines to assist in the prevention of heart disease. A pleasurable diet, low in fats and meats, and high in seasonally fresh vegetables, fruits, fishes and grains has also been shown to have numerous other health benefits.

These recipes have been adapted to meet the guidelines of the American Heart Association. Although all recipes are reduced in fat and cholesterol, those such as chocolate desserts should not be eaten every day, but may be enjoyed once or twice a week. A heart-healthy diet includes diverse and good-tasting dishes that are reasonably low in fat, served in average size proportions, employing common sense meal plans, and regular exercise.

The Hints and References section has specific guidelines for a heart-healthy diet. Also shown is data on the fats and cholesterol found in oils. Although the sodium and sugars in these recipes has been reduced or removed, people on strict diets should adapt recipes to their individual needs.

Please take a few minutes and explore the resources in this book. It has been carefully written to offer you the best of Coastal New England Cooking.

This book is dedicated to
Eliot Brye,

who showed me that the most
creative and magical kitchen to work in
begins with the least amount of food.

CREDITS:

Cover: "Canterbury Manor" from cotton print, gratefully used as a courtesy of:
Hoffman International Fabrics

Cover Designs, Layout and Typesetting: Sherri Eldridge

Front Cover Nautical and Back Cover Watercolors, Chapter Title Page Art:
Robert Groves, Brooksville, Maine

Text Line Sketches: Robert Groves and Nadine Pranckunas

Proofreading: Marcie Correa, Bill Eldridge, Eleanor Rhinelander and Ellen Bowlin

Support, Patience and Recipes: Bill Eldridge, Fran Goldberg, The LeForestiers,
Annie Shaw and the Women's Business Development Corporation

CONTENTS

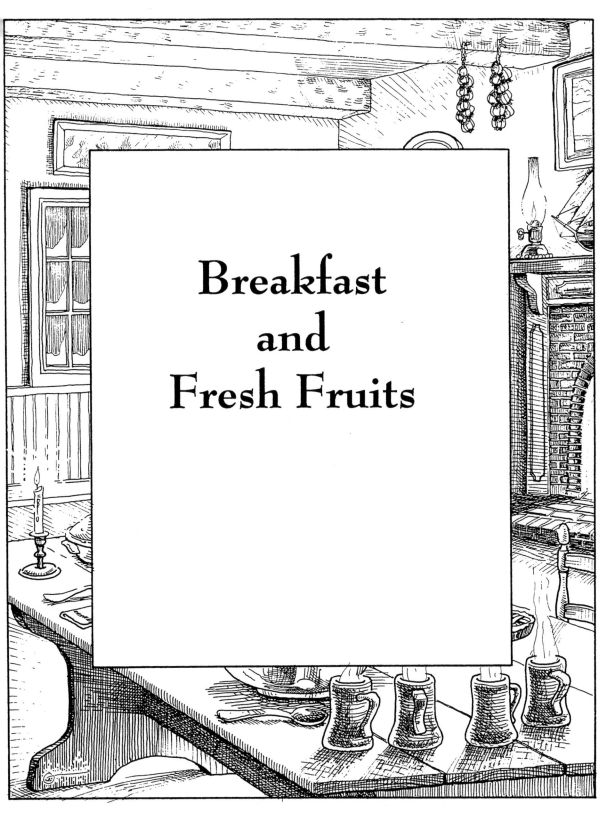

Breakfast
and
Fresh Fruits

COASTAL NEW ENGLAND   WINTERFARE COOKING

CONTENTS

For other breakfast foods, please refer to the chapters
"Breads and Baked Goods" and "Desserts and Sweets."

COASTAL NEW ENGLAND   WINTERFARE COOKING

Banana-Fruit Smoothie

3 bananas
$^3/_4$ cup drained and
    chopped peaches
    in unsweetened juice
$^1/_2$ cup unsweetened
    applesauce
1 cup non-fat plain
    yogurt
1 cup orange juice
3 tablespoons frozen juice
    concentrate, any kind
$^1/_4$ cup honey
2 teaspoons lemon juice

SERVES 2-3

Chop bananas into 1-inch pieces. Place all ingredients in blender and whip 1 minute, or until smooth.

3

A Bowl of Ambrosia

A cheery fruit medley to brighten any cold winter morning.

3 large navel oranges
3 ripe bananas
$1/_2$ cup fresh pineapple
      pieces, or unsweetened
      canned pineapple
$1/_4$ cup honey or sugar
1 cup shredded coconut
4 tablespoons orange juice
cherries or strawberries
      for garnish (optional)

SERVES 4

Carefully peel and remove membranes from orange sections, leaving sections whole.

Cut bananas into bite-sized pieces. Combine bananas with pineapple, honey or sugar, and shredded coconut.

Arrange alternate layers of oranges and banana/pineapple mixture in individual serving dishes. Over the top of each bowl of ambrosia, sprinkle 1 tablespoon orange juice. Chill well before serving. Garnish with a cherry or strawberry.

COASTAL NEW ENGLAND   WINTERFARE COOKING

Broiled Fruits with Spiced Honey

1 cup cranberry sauce or
    raspberry jam
2 teaspoons butter
2 tablespoons honey
1 tablespoon cinnamon
pinch of salt
2 cans peaches, apricots,
    pineapple and/or
    pears in unsweetened
    juice

SERVES 4

Put cranberry sauce or raspberry jam in small saucepan with butter, honey, cinnamon and salt. Cook for 10 minutes over medium heat, stirring frequently to avoid sticking.

Spray baking pan with non-stick vegetable oil. Place fruits on baking pan (peaches, pears and apricots hollow-side up.) Coat by brushing a thick layer of sauce over each fruit.

Place under broiler, watching closely, until lightly brown. Broiled fruits make a pretty presentation by themselves or over pancakes.

Honey producers in New England are often travelling apiaries. The beekeeper, with his bees and hives, travels from field to field to pollinate different crops. The delicate scent of the blossoms is transmitted to the honey the bees then produce, for example, "blueberry" or "apple" honey has been made by bees while they pollinate those crops.

Chilled Prunes in Wine

1¹/₂ cups dried pitted
    prunes
1 cup water
¹/₂ cup dry sherry or port
1 tablespoon sugar
5 thin seeded lemon slices
1 cup canned or fresh
    roasted chestnut
    meats (optional)

SERVES 4-6

Cover prunes with cold water and sherry or port. Bring to a boil in a medium saucepan. Reduce heat and simmer 2 minutes. Mix in sugar and lemon slices. Cook 3 minutes more, then remove from heat.

Place in covered jar and chill at least 4 hours.

Just before serving, prunes may be stuffed with chestnut meats. Serve cold or briefly heat in oven dish.

Chestnuts have relatively little fat compared to other nuts. Three ounces of roasted chestnuts contain less than 1 gram of fat, while three ounces of assorted dry roasted nuts have over 45 grams of fat!

COASTAL NEW ENGLAND   WINTERFARE COOKING

Apple-Walnut Pancakes

2 cups all-purpose flour
5 teaspoons baking
    powder
1 teaspoon salt
3 teaspoons sugar
3 eggs, separated
1 cup unsweetened
    applesauce
1 cup skim milk
3 tablespoons canola oil
$1/4$ cup chopped walnuts

SERVES 4

Sift together all dry ingredients. In a separate bowl beat egg yolks, applesauce, milk and oil.

Whip egg whites into soft peaks and gently fold into batter. Stir in chopped walnuts. Pour one-third cup batter per pancake.

Apple Maple Syrup

1 cup maple syrup
3 tablespoons frozen apple
    juice concentrate
3 inch cinnamon stick

Put all ingredients together in saucepan and simmer on medium heat for 15 minutes. Remove cinnamon stick and serve warm over pancakes or waffles.

Buckwheat Ployes

SERVES 4

1 cup buckwheat flour
$^1/_2$ cup all-purpose flour
1 teaspoon baking powder
$^1/_2$ teaspoon baking soda
1 teaspoon sugar
1 egg
$1^1/_4$ cups skim milk
2 tablespoons non-fat sour
   cream or plain yogurt
2 tablespoons canola oil

Sift dry ingredients into medium-sized bowl. In a separate bowl, whip wet ingredients. Combine mixtures and beat until smooth.

Spray hot griddle with non-stick oil. Ladle out 3 tablespoons batter. Using circular motion with back of spoon, spread to $^1/_8$ inch thick. Cook $1^1/_2$ minutes on just one side.

Apricot Butter

2 cups dried apricots
$1^1/_2$ cups apple cider
1 teaspoon lemon juice
1 teaspoon nutmeg

Chop apricots into small pieces. Simmer apricots in cider about 20 minutes (add more cider if needed). Stir in lemon juice and nutmeg. Purée in blender or food processor.

French-style Canadian buckwheat pancakes, called "Ployes," have long been a staple in the northern Maine woods and coastal towns. They are thin and can be rolled up with jams, syrup, spreads, caviar or smoked fish. Ployes are viewed as a bread and can be served at any meal. They freeze well and can be quickly reheated in an oven just before serving.

COASTAL NEW ENGLAND   WINTERFARE COOKING

Winter Squash Waffles

SERVES 3-4

$^1/_2$ cup winter squash,
    boiled and mashed
2 eggs
$1^1/_2$ cups skim milk
3 tablespoons canola oil
1 cup all-purpose flour
4 teaspoons double-acting
    baking powder
1 tablespoon sugar
$^1/_4$ teaspoon cinnamon
$^1/_4$ teaspoon nutmeg
2 egg whites

Mix together mashed winter squash, whole eggs, milk and oil.

In a separate bowl, sift together the dry ingredients. Stir into winter squash mixture.

Beat egg whites until soft peaks form. Gently fold whites into batter. Cook in preheated waffle griddle sprayed with non-stick oil.

Honey-Clove Syrup

1 cup honey
$^1/_4$ cup water
12 whole cloves

Put honey and water in small saucepan over medium heat. Tie cloves in cheesecloth and place in saucepan. Simmer for 15 minutes, then remove spice bag. Serve warm.

COASTAL NEW ENGLAND   WINTERFARE COOKING

Lemon Waffles

1 cup all-purpose flour
2 tablespoons baking
   powder
$^1/_4$ cup sugar
$^1/_2$ teaspoon baking soda
2 eggs, separated
$^1/_2$ cup skim milk
$^1/_2$ cup club soda
3 tablespoons finely
   grated lemon rind
1 teaspoon vanilla extract
3 tablespoons canola oil

SERVES 4

Sift together dry ingredients. In a separate bowl, whip together egg yolks and all other ingredients, except egg whites.

Beat egg whites to soft peaks and gently fold into batter. Spray preheated waffle griddle with non-stick cooking oil. Spray again before ladling out batter for each waffle.

Lemon-Lime Whipped Glaze

$2^1/_2$ cups confectioner's
   sugar
$^1/_4$ cup lemon juice
$^1/_4$ cup lime juice
2 teaspoons vanilla
2 egg whites

Combine all ingredients, except egg whites, and whip together with electric beater. In a separate bowl, whip egg whites, then gently fold into glaze. Serve as sauce over waffles.

COASTAL NEW ENGLAND   WINTERFARE COOKING

Sweet Egg Kugel

8 oz. medium uncooked
  egg noodles
$^3/_4$ cup sugar
2 tablespoons cinnamon
$^1/_2$ lb. non-fat cottage
  cheese
2 tablespoons melted
  butter
1 teaspoon vanilla extract
4 eggs
1 cup skim milk
8 oz. non-fat cream
  cheese
$1^1/_2$ cups non-fat sour
  cream

SERVES 8

Boil noodles until tender, but firm to the bite. Drain. In a mixing bowl, whip together $^1/_2$-cup sugar, 1 tablespoon cinnamon and remaining ingredients.

Stir in noodles by hand. Pour into casserole sprayed with non-stick oil. Mix together remaining $^1/_4$-cup sugar and 1 tablespoon cinnamon. Sprinkle over top of casserole.

Bake in 350° oven until browned, about 50 minutes. Serve hot.

COASTAL NEW ENGLAND   WINTERFARE COOKING

Herbed Cheddar Omelette

2 large eggs
1 teaspoon water
pinch of salt
fresh ground pepper
$1/_2$ teaspoon dill
$1/_2$ teaspoon parsley
$1/_2$ teaspoon chopped
   chives
1 tablespoon grated
   low-fat Cheddar
   cheese

MAKES ONE OMELETTE
Multiply ingredients by number of omelettes.

Mix together herbs in a small bowl. Set near stove with grated cheese.

Preheat 8-10 inch, non-stick omelette pan over high heat. Whisk eggs, water, salt and pepper together in bowl. Just before pouring eggs into pan, spray with non-stick vegetable oil. Pour eggs into middle of pan ($1/_2$-cup at a time if using a number of eggs.) Shake and swirl pan to distribute eggs evenly. Rest on heat 5 seconds to firm the bottom, while sprinkling herbs and cheese on top.

Note: Have spatula handy to assist omelette in its formative stages. An omelette should be cooked in just 20-30 seconds!

Hold pan by its handle and jerk quickly towards you while tilting far edge over burner. Continue this process and omelette will roll over on itself. When omelette forms at far end, bang on handle near pan to curl edge.

COASTAL NEW ENGLAND   WINTERFARE COOKING

Apple Jelly Roll

2 cups all-purpose flour
2 teaspoons baking
powder
2 teaspoons sugar
2 cups skim milk
3 large eggs
2 tablespoons canola oil
1¹/₂ cups peeled and
grated apples
1 teaspoon lemon juice
¹/₂ cup sugar
1 teaspoon cinnamon
1 tablespoon water
2 teaspoons cornstarch

To Serve: Roll each jelly roll with 2 tablespoons apple sauce. Sprinkle the tops with a blend of cinnamon and sugar.

MAKES EIGHT 8-INCH JELLY ROLLS

Sift flour before measuring. Mix flour with baking powder and 2 teaspoons sugar. Whisk in milk, eggs and oil. Blend until perfectly smooth. Rest in refrigerator 30 minutes.

In a covered saucepan over medium-low heat, simmer grated apples, lemon juice, ¹/₂ cup sugar and cinnamon for 10 minutes. Blend cornstarch and water, then add to apples. Cook until thickened. Keep warm.

Preheat 8-inch pan over medium-high heat. Spray with non-stick cooking oil and quickly pour ¹/₃ cup of batter in middle of pan, tilt to cover. Bottom will be lightly brown in 30 seconds, then flip and cook 20 seconds on second side.

COASTAL NEW ENGLAND   WINTERFARE COOKING

Fruited Breakfast Pudding

4 cups water
2 cups couscous
$1^1/_2$ cups skim milk
1 tablespoon butter
5 tablespoons sugar
pinch of salt
1 teaspoon ground
    cinnamon
1 teaspoon vanilla
1 teaspoon lemon juice
2 eggs
2 egg whites
$^1/_2$ cup dried apricots
    or apples

SERVES 8

Preheat oven to 325°.

Boil water, then add couscous. Reduce heat to low and cover. The couscous will absorb the water in about 5 minutes.

In a mixing bowl, beat together all the other ingredients, except the dried fruit. Stir in couscous, then the dried fruit. Mix well.

Pour into baking dish sprayed with non-stick oil. If desired, sprinkle tops with additional cinnamon and sugar. Bake 45 minutes. Pudding can be served warm or cold.

Herbal Christmas Wreath: To a spruce or pine fir wreath, add sprigs of dried opal basil, winter savory, cinnamon sticks, anise-hyssop, bee balm, white peppermint blossoms, hydrangea and colored sage. These herbs can also be hung in small bunches from the tree, used to make a holiday center-piece or pomander balls.

Cornmeal Mush

2 cups boiling skim milk
2 cups boiling water
1 cup cornmeal
$^1/_2$ cup cold water
pinch of salt
maple syrup or molasses

SERVES 4

Fill bottom pan of a double boiler with water and bring to a boil. In the top pan, pour in 2 cups each boiling milk and water.

In a mixing bowl, stir together cornmeal, $^1/_2$ cup cold water and salt. Slowly add cornmeal mixture to hot liquids in double boiler. Stir over boiling water for 3 minutes. Reduce heat to moderate, cover and cook 30 minutes more, stirring frequently.

Serve in bowls with maple syrup or molasses.

COASTAL NEW ENGLAND   WINTERFARE COOKING

Maple Walnut Oatmeal

This recipe is made with whole rolled oats, not the quick variety.
The flavor and texture far surpasses processed oatmeal.

2³/₄ cups water
1 cup skim milk
pinch of salt
1 cup whole rolled oats
2 tablespoons chopped
    walnuts
maple syrup

SERVES 2

Boil water, milk and salt. Add rolled oats. Cook 10 minutes, stirring occasionally. Cover pot, remove from heat, and let stand about 5 minutes.

Serve each bowl of oatmeal with 1 tablespoon of chopped walnuts, and maple syrup to taste.

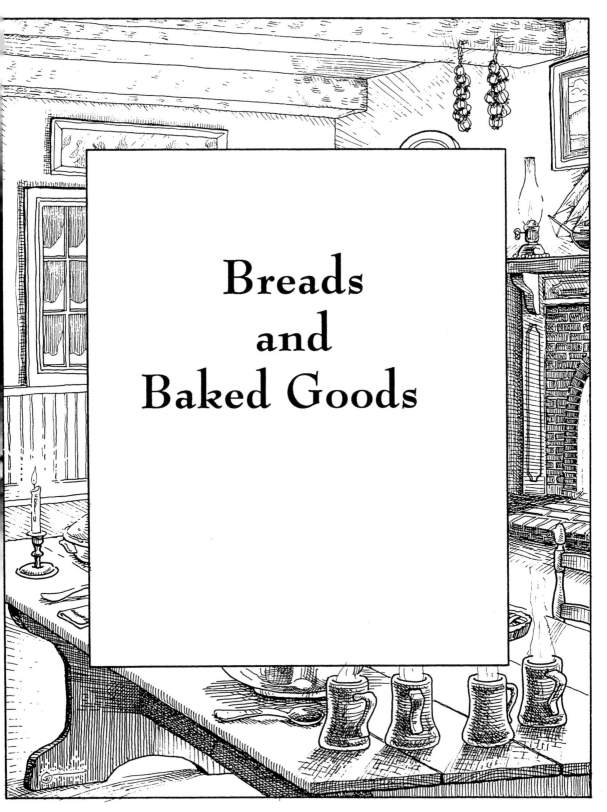

Breads
and
Baked Goods

CONTENTS

Sweet baked goods are also in the chapter "Desserts and Sweets."
Spreads for bread are located in "Appetizers and Finger Food."

COASTAL NEW ENGLAND   WINTERFARE COOKING

Cranberry-Orange Muffins

MAKES 12 MUFFINS

1 cup chopped fresh
    or frozen cranberries
$^1/_2$ cup sugar
$1^3/_4$ cups all-purpose flour
pinch of salt
2 teaspoons double-acting
    baking powder
1 teaspoon cinnamon
1 teaspoon ground ginger
1 egg
$^1/_4$ cup canola oil
$^1/_2$ cup orange juice
$^1/_4$ cup skim milk
1 tablespoon finely grated
    orange rind

Preheat oven to 400°. Spray muffin tins with non-stick oil.

Mix cranberries with sugar and set aside. Sift together flour, salt, baking powder and spices. In a separate bowl, beat together remaining ingredients. With a few swift strokes, briefly stir mixtures together and add cranberries (some lumps will remain.)

Fill muffin tins two-thirds full. Bake 20 minutes, or until a toothpick inserted in the center of muffins comes out clean.

Raisin-Yam Bran Muffins

A tongue-twister of a name, guaranteed easier to eat than to say.

1$^1/_2$ cups all-purpose flour
$^1/_2$ teaspoon salt
2 teaspoons baking
    powder
1 teaspoon baking soda
1 teaspoon ground cloves
1 teaspoon cinnamon
$^1/_2$ cup bran flakes
1$^1/_4$ cups brown sugar
$^1/_2$ cup skim milk
2 eggs
3 tablespoons canola oil
1 cup cold cooked
    mashed yams or
    sweet potatoes
$^1/_2$ cup raisins

MAKES 20-24 MUFFINS

Preheat oven to 350°. Spray muffin tins with non-stick oil.

Sift together flour, salt, baking powder, baking soda and spices. Stir in bran flakes. In a separate bowl, beat together brown sugar, milk, eggs and oil. Blend in mashed yams. Slowly add dry ingredients to yam mixture. Beat well, so batter is smooth.

Fill muffin tins two-thirds full. Bake 20-25 minutes, or until toothpick inserted in the center of muffins comes out clean.

COASTAL NEW ENGLAND   WINTERFARE COOKING

Buttermilk Pineapple Muffins

2 cups sifted all-purpose
    flour
2 teaspoons double-acting
    baking powder
$1/2$ teaspoon baking soda
pinch of salt
2 tablespoons sugar
1 cup low-fat buttermilk
1 egg, beaten
$1/4$ cup skim milk
3 tablespoons canola oil
$1/2$ cup crushed pineapple,
    drained well

MAKES 12 MUFFINS

Preheat oven to 400°. Spray muffin tins with non-stick oil.

Sift together flour, baking powder, baking soda and salt.

In a separate bowl, beat together sugar, buttermilk, egg, milk and oil. Briefly stir both mixtures together, adding pineapple at the same time. Batter will be lumpy.

Spoon into muffin tins. Bake 25 minutes, or until a toothpick inserted in the center of muffins comes out clean.

New England Woods Potpourri: Combine 1 cup cedar tips, 1 cup sweet woodruff, 1 cup sandalwood chips, and 1 cup hawthorn or juniper berries. Mix well and scent with 4 drops green forest or pine oil.

Fluffy Biscuits

2 cups sifted all-purpose
   flour
2 teaspoons baking
   powder
$1/2$ teaspoon baking soda
1 teaspoon sugar
pinch of salt
$1/2$ cup canola oil
$3/4$ cup cold low-fat
   buttermilk

MAKES 12 BISCUITS

Set rack in middle of oven. Preheat to 450°. Spray cookie sheet with non-stick oil.

Mix flour, baking powder, baking soda, sugar and salt together. Slowly add oil, and use a butter knife to "cut" oil into flour mixture until evenly distributed.

Stir in buttermilk. Batter should form a somewhat sticky ball, or add just enough buttermilk to make it hold together. Flour your hands, divide dough, and shape into biscuits. Place on cookie sheet and bake 10-12 minutes.

COASTAL NEW ENGLAND   WINTERFARE COOKING

Oatmeal Rolls

1 cup rolled oats (not
   quick oats)
$^1/_2$ tablespoon canola oil
$^1/_2$ teaspoon salt
$1^1/_2$ cups boiling water
1 tablespoon very hot
   water
1 pkg. active dry yeast
$^1/_2$ cup molasses or honey
4 cups sifted all-purpose
   flour

MAKES 3 DOZEN ROLLS

Boil water in bottom pan of a double boiler. In the top pan, combine oats, oil, salt and $1^1/_2$ cups boiling water. Cook for 1 hour, stirring occasionally. Cool until lukewarm.

In a small cup, blend the tablespoon of very hot water with yeast. Stir yeast mixture into cooked oats. Add molasses or honey and flour. Knead until well blended. Cover, and let rise until double in bulk, about 2 hours.

Spray muffin tins with non-stick oil. With oiled hands, pinch off pieces of dough and place in tins. Let rise again until double in bulk. Bake in 425° oven for 20 minutes.

Pretzels

1 cup 105°-115° water
1 pkg. active dry yeast
2³/₄ cups all-purpose flour
2 tablespoons soft butter
¹/₂ teaspoon salt
1 tablespoon sugar
4 cups water
5 teaspoons baking soda
Optional:
coarse salt or sea salt

MAKES TWELVE 6-INCH PRETZELS

Combine 1 cup warm water and yeast. Let set 5 minutes, stir until dissolved. Add 1¹/₂-cups of the flour, butter, salt and sugar. Beat at least 3 minutes. Stir in remaining 1¹/₄ cup flour and knead until dough is no longer sticky. Cover, and let rise in bowl until double in bulk. Punch down and divide into 12 equal pieces. Roll pieces between palms into 18" pencil-thin lengths. Spray cookie sheet with non-stick oil. Loop into twisted oval pretzel shape. Place on cookie sheet and let rise until almost double in bulk. Boil water with baking soda in a non-aluminum pot. One at a time, gently remove pretzels with slotted spatula and lower into boiling water for 1 minute or until they float. Return to cookie sheet, sprinkle with salt, if desired. Bake in 475° oven 10-12 minutes.

COASTAL NEW ENGLAND   WINTERFARE COOKING

French Onion Sticks

$3^1/_4$ cups flour
1 tablespoon sugar
pinch of salt
1 pkg. active dry yeast
1 cup warm water
6 tablespoons olive oil
1 cup grated onions

MAKES 24 STICKS

Combine 1 cup of the flour with sugar, salt and yeast. Add water, beating until smooth. Mix in 3 tablespoons of the olive oil and $1^1/_4$-cups more flour. Beat well. Turn onto board, knead in remaining flour. Continue kneading until smooth (add flour if dough is sticky). Place in bowl sprayed with non-stick oil, turning to coat all sides. Cover, let rise until double in bulk. Punch down. Saute onions in 2 tablespoons olive oil. Knead onions into dough, then divide into 24 balls. Roll balls between palms to form sticks. Place on cookie sheet sprayed with non-stick oil. Brush sticks with olive oil. Let rise until double in bulk. Bake in 400° oven 12-15 minutes.

Egg Challah
This easy bread is healthy and beautiful.
Serve whole and warm, inviting everyone to twist off a piece of the braid.

2 pkgs. active dry yeast
1 teaspoon sugar
$^1/_4$ cup very warm water
6 cups all-purpose flour
1 teaspoon salt
2 cups very warm water
3 eggs, slightly beaten
$^1/_4$ cup canola oil
3 tablespoons sugar
2 cups flour for kneading
1 egg yolk
2 tablespoons skim milk
4 tablespoons poppy seeds

MAKES 2 LOAVES

With a small whisk, beat yeast, 1 teaspoon sugar and $^1/_4$ cup very warm water. In large bowl combine 6 cups flour and salt. Make a deep well in center of the flour, pour in yeast mixture. Add eggs, oil and remaining sugar. Beat well, then turn onto floured board. Knead until dough is smooth and elastic. Place in bowl sprayed with vegetable oil, turning to coat all sides. Cover, and let rise until double in bulk. Punch down, knead briefly, then divide in half. Cut each half into 3 sections. Roll sections into 18-inch long tapered ropes. Place the 3 ropes side-by-side on a cookie sheet (sprayed with non-stick oil). Starting in the middle, braid ropes to both ends and tuck ends under. Cover, rise until double in bulk. Brush tops with egg yolk beaten with skim milk, sprinkle with poppy seeds. Bake at 400° 15 minutes, reduce to 375° and bake 20 minutes more.

Low-Fat Basic Bread

1 cup warm water
2 tablespoons sugar
1 pkg. active dry yeast
$^1/_2$ teaspoon sea salt
2 tablespoons safflower
   oil
2 tablespoons sesame
   seeds
3 cups unbleached flour

Kneading:
1-2 cups flour

Loaf Crusts:
3 tablespoons sesame
   seeds
1 tablespoon skim milk

MAKES 2 LOAVES

In a large bowl, combine water, sugar and yeast. Let rest 5 minutes, then stir. Mix in remaining ingredients in order listed. Knead about 10 minutes, working in additional flour. Spray a bowl with vegetable oil. Place dough in bowl, turn to coat all sides. Cover, and let rise until double in bulk.

Spray two 9" x 5" bread pans with non-stick oil. Dust each pan with a tablespoon of sesame seeds. Punch down dough and shape into two 9-inch loaves. Place in pans. Brush milk over the tops and sprinkle with remaining sesame seeds. Cover, let rise until double in bulk. Bake in 400° oven 30 minutes.

Safflower oil, a healthy oil very low in saturated fat, was considered the least desirable of oils in Old World cooking. Even in India, only the poorest people benefited by using safflower oil. Historically, the healthier, natural food products have been left for the poor, as in China where only the lowest citizens once ate whole grain brown rice.

COASTAL NEW ENGLAND   WINTERFARE COOKING

Swedish Buttermilk Rye Bread

$^1/_2$ cup very warm water
2 pkgs. active dry yeast
1 cup low-fat buttermilk
$^1/_2$ cup molasses
3 tablespoons canola oil
1 teaspoon salt
2 tablespoons finely
    grated orange rind
2 tablespoons caraway
    seeds
$2^1/_2$ cups finely milled rye
    flour, sifted
3 cups all-purpose flour,
    plus flour for
    kneading
1 tablespoon skim milk
2 teaspoons caraway
    seeds

MAKES 2 LOAVES

In a large bowl, dissolve yeast in water. In a small saucepan, warm buttermilk, molasses and oil, then add to yeast mixture. Mix in salt, grated rind and 2 tablespoons caraway seeds. Stir in flours. Turn out and knead 10 minutes on floured board. Spray another bowl with vegetable oil. Place dough in bowl, turn to coat all sides. Cover, and let rise until double in bulk.

Spray two 9" x 5" bread pans with non-stick oil. Punch down dough, and shape into two 9-inch loaves. Place in pans. With a very sharp knife, make four $^1/_4$-inch deep slashes in the tops of the loaves. Brush milk over the tops and sprinkle with remaining caraway seeds. Cover, let rise until double in bulk. Bake in 375° oven 30-35 minutes.

COASTAL NEW ENGLAND   WINTERFARE COOKING

Potato Bread

$^3/_4$ cup very warm water
1 teaspoon sugar
2 pkgs. active dry yeast
$1^1/_2$ cup mashed potatoes
$1^1/_2$ cups low-fat
    buttermilk
4 tablespoons melted
    butter
$^1/_2$ cup honey
2 teaspoons salt
2 cups oat, rice or whole
    wheat flour
$^1/_2$ cup wheat germ
$4^1/_2$ cups all-purpose flour

MAKES 3 LOAVES

Dissolve the yeast and sugar in water. In a large bowl, mix mashed potatoes, buttermilk, butter, honey and salt. Beat for 2 minutes, then add yeast mixture. Stir in oat, rice or wheat flour, wheat germ and 2 cups all-purpose flour. Turn onto floured board and work in remaining flour. Knead 8 minutes, adding flour as needed to keep dough from sticking. Place in bowl sprayed with non-stick oil, turn dough to coat all sides. Cover, and let rise until double in bulk. Punch down, then shape into 3 loaves. Place each loaf in a 9" x 5" bread pan that's been sprayed with non-stick oil. Let rise until double in bulk. Bake in 375° oven 30-35 minutes.

Sourdough Brown Bread

Sourdough Starter:
1 pkg. active dry yeast
2 cups lukewarm water
2 cups all-pourpose flour
1 tablespoon dark
    molasses

Sourdough:
1 cup sourdough starter
$^1/_2$ cup low-fat buttermilk
1 cup dark molasses
2 tablespoons sugar
$^3/_4$ teaspoon salt
2 cups graham flour
2 cups sifted all-purpose
    flour

MAKES 9" x 5" LOAF

Sourdough Starter: Combine all ingredients in a wide-mouthed crockery or glass jar. Stir with a wooden spoon (never metal.) Leave uncovered at 80° for 4-7 days. Stir down each day and whenever a crust forms. Starter is ready for use, or storage in the refrigerator, when it bubbles and emits a sour odor.

In a large mixing bowl, stir sourdough ingredients, one at a time, into sourdough starter in the order they are listed.

Spray a 9" x 5" bread pan with non-stick oil. Pour batter into pan and let rise until double in bulk. Bake in 350° oven 1 hour or bread sounds hollow when tapped.

COASTAL NEW ENGLAND   WINTERFARE COOKING

Quick Pumpkin-Orange Bread

1 cup cooked or canned
  mashed pumpkin
1 cup sugar
$^1/_2$ cup brown sugar
$^1/_3$ cup canola oil
1 egg
1 egg white
$^1/_2$ cup orange juice
1 teaspoon vanilla extract
$1^3/_4$ cups all-purpose flour
1 teaspoon baking powder
1 teaspoon baking soda
$^1/_2$ teaspoon cinnamon
$^1/_2$ teaspoon ground cloves
Optional:
$^1/_2$ cup chopped dates

MAKES ONE 9" x 5" LOAF

Preheat oven to 350°. Beat together mashed pumpkin, sugars, oil, eggs, orange juice and vanilla. Sift together dry ingredients. Very briefly stir the dry mixture into the pumpkin blend, with just a few strokes. Quickly stir in chopped dates, if desired.

Spray a 9" x 5" bread pan, or two mini pans, with non-stick oil. Pour batter into pan, bake 50 minutes (less for mini-pans). Remove from oven when toothpick inserted in center of bread comes out clean. Leave in pan 10 minutes before turning onto wire rack to cool.

Hot Cross Buns

1 cup skim milk
$^1/_4$ cup sugar
$^1/_2$ teaspoon cinnamon
1 tablespoon finely grated
    orange rind
$^1/_2$ cup currants or raisins
2 tablespoons butter
$^1/_2$ teaspoon salt
1 pkg. active dry yeast
2 tablespoons hot water
1 egg
$2^2/_3$ cup all-purpose flour

Milk Glaze:
$^3/_4$ cup confectioner's
    sugar, sifted
2 tablespoons hot milk
$^1/_2$ teaspoon vanilla

MAKES 18 BUNS

Scald milk. Remove from heat. Add sugar, cinnamon, grated orange rind, currants or raisins, butter and salt.

In a separate bowl, sprinkle yeast over hot (not boiling) water. Rest 5 minutes, then stir milk mixture into yeast mixture. Beat in egg. Mix in most of the flour, then knead in the rest. Place in bowl, cover with floured towel, and let rise until double in bulk.

Preheat oven to 425°. Spray large cake pan with non-stick vegetable oil. Punch down dough and roll into 18 balls. Place in prepared pan and press down to flatten buns. Cover, and let rise until double in bulk. Bake at 400° for 20 minutes, or until light golden. Mix confectioner's sugar with hot milk and vanilla. Drizzle over buns in classic cross pattern, or swirl over top of each.

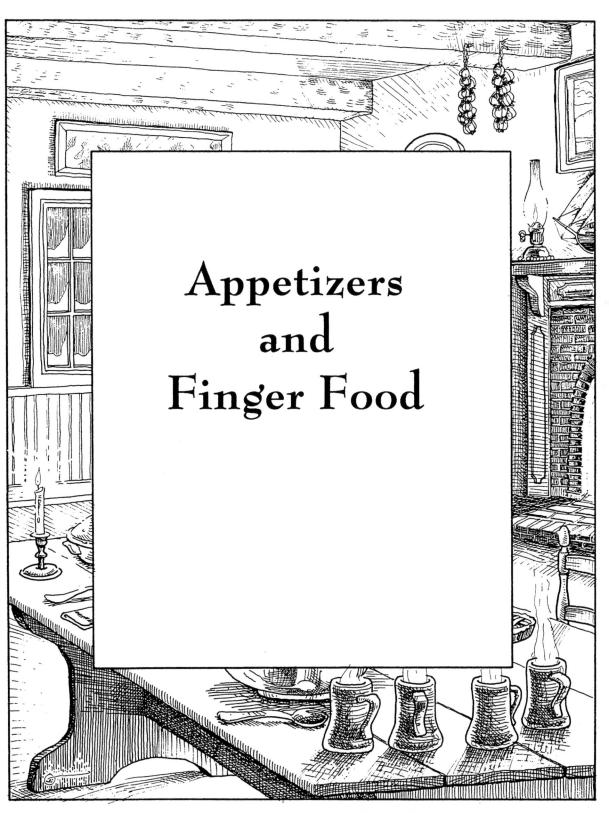

Appetizers
and
Finger Food

COASTAL NEW ENGLAND   WINTERFARE COOKING

CONTENTS

Appetizers can be used as a main dish by doubling the amount of food per serving.

COASTAL NEW ENGLAND   WINTERFARE COOKING

Shrimp and Lobster Remoulade

2 lbs. large cooked shrimp,
peeled and deveined

8 oz. cooked lobster meat,
cut in bite-sized pieces

1 cup non-fat mayonnaise

$\frac{1}{3}$ cup chili sauce

1 teaspoon grated onion

1 tablespoon parsley

1 tablespoon
Worcestershire sauce

1 teaspoon horseradish

1 teaspoon sweet pickle
relish

1 teaspoon Dijon mustard

1 tablespoon capers,
rinsed and drained

SERVES 10

Toss shrimp and lobster meat together. Chill.

In a large mixing bowl, blend all remaining ingredients.   Gently fold in shrimp and lobster. Place in a serving bowl. Cover with plastic wrap and refrigerate at least a few hours, but preferably overnight.

Serve with cocktail forks or on appetizer plates. Your guests will love you for this!

**View from Cadillac Mountain
Mount Desert Island, Maine**

Oysters Rockefeller

30 medium-sized oysters
  on the half shell
rock salt to set oysters on
2 bags spinach, cooked
  and well drained
¼ cup onion,
  finely chopped
2 tablespoons olive oil
2 tablespoons soft butter
½ cup dry bread crumbs
1 tablespoon parsley
6 drops hot pepper sauce

Optional:
2 teaspoons anisette

SERVES 6

Preheat oven to 475°. Pour rock salt in baking dishes, at least 1 inch thick. Embed oysters in the rock salt, sunny-side up, to balance and protect them from overcooking.

Press moisture out of spinach, so it is quite dry. Chop very fine. Sauté onion in olive oil. Mix spinach, onion and butter in bowl, then add remaining ingredients. Spread mixture on oysters. Bake in oven 10 minutes or until plump, then broil until browned. Serve hot.

Artifacts recently found at Bull Brook in Ipswich, Massachusetts, suggest that the first people came to the New England coastal region around 8,000 B.C. Their ancestors had crossed the land bridge over the Bering Sea 20,000 years ago, and their decedents left enormous oyster piles on the banks of the Damariscotta and Kennebec Rivers in Maine.

COASTAL NEW ENGLAND   WINTERFARE COOKING

Asparagus Cheese Puffs

1 cup cooked asparagus,
    fresh, frozen or
    canned
2 egg whites
2 tablespoons softened
    low-fat cream cheese
3 tablespoons grated
    Parmesan cheese
3 tablespoons non-fat
    mayonnaise
1 teaspoon paprika
pinch of curry
pinch of salt
pinch of pepper
crackers or Melba toast
    rounds

SERVES 4

Preheat broiler. Coarsely mash asparagus.

Beat egg whites until stiff. In a separate bowl, blend together cream cheese, Parmesan, mayonnaise and spices. Fold egg whites into cheese mixture. Gently add asparagus. Heap onto crackers or Melba toast rounds. Set on cookie sheet. Watch closely under broiler, remove when puffs are light gold. Serve hot.

Vegetable Spring Rolls

Like all of America's immigrants, those recently arriving from Asia have enhanced the local cuisine. These spring rolls use local winter vegetables.

$^1/_2$ cup cider vinegar
6 tablespoons sugar
pinch of cayenne
$^1/_2$ teaspoon salt
1 garlic clove, minced
2 cups fresh bean sprouts
2 cups shredded Chinese
    cabbage
1 cup thinly sliced carrots
1 tablespoon grated onion
$^1/_2$ cup slivered water
    chestnuts
1 tablespoon cornstarch
8 spring-roll or egg-roll
    wrappers
canola oil for frying

SERVES 8

Whisk vinegar and sugar together in a large mixing bowl. Stir in spices, sprouts, cabbage, carrots, onion and water chestnuts. Let sit for one hour, then drain in a colander. Return to bowl, mix in powdered cornstarch.

Fill and roll up spring-roll or egg-roll wrappers according to manufacturer's instructions. Pour 1 inch of canola oil into frying pan and set on medium-high heat. It will take about 7 minutes before oil is hot enough. Carefully place rolls in hot oil, and turn constantly until browned on all sides (about 5-6 minutes). Drain on paper towels.

COASTAL NEW ENGLAND   WINTERFARE COOKING

Crab Toasts

1 lb. crab meat
pinch of salt
1 tablespoon sherry
1 scallion, chopped fine
1 egg, beaten
3 tablespoons almond
     slivers
$^1/_2$ teaspoon ginger
1 tablespoon cornstarch
6 slices white bread
canola oil for frying

MAKES 2 DOZEN

Mix together crab meat, salt, sherry, scallion, egg, almond slivers, ginger and cornstarch. Let mixture rest 15 mintues.

Spray a large frying pan with non-stick oil. Pour $^1/_4$ inch canola oil into pan and preheat on medium-high.

Trim crust from bread slices, then cut each piece into four triangles. Spread each triangle with 1 tablespoon crab mixture. Fry, crab side down, until golden brown. Remove with slotted spatula and drain on paper towels.

COASTAL NEW ENGLAND   WINTERFARE COOKING

Marinated Shrimp with Artichoke Hearts

1¹/₂ lbs. large shrimp, cooked, peeled and deveined

8-oz. can artichoke hearts

12 mushrooms

1 sweet onion (Vidalia or purple) sliced in rings

12 pitted black olives

3¹/₂-oz. jar drained capers

1 pint cherry tomatoes

Marinade:

1 cup safflower oil

³/₄ cup cider vinegar

3 tablespoons Worcestershire sauce

2 teaspoons Tabasco

1 tablespoon sugar

salt and pepper to taste

SERVES 8

Place shrimp in a wide shallow container. Chop artichoke hearts into bite-sized pieces; mushrooms in half to show shape; onion into thin rings; and olives into round halves. Mix together all vegetables, including tomatoes, with shrimp.

In a separate bowl, mix marinade ingredients. Pour over shrimp and vegetables. Cover container and chill for at least 24 hours, stirring occasionally.

Drain off marinade before serving.

COASTAL NEW ENGLAND   WINTERFARE COOKING

Pickled Oysters or Mussels

1 peck oysters or mussels
1 quart oyster liquor,
    clam juice and/or
    vegetable broth
1 tablespoon peppercorns
1 tablespoon allspice
1 thinly sliced lemon
1 tablespoon vinegar
1 teaspoon minced garlic

SERVES 4

Thoroughly scrub oysters or mussels, discarding any that do not close. In a large pot, cook oysters or mussels in the liquid until shells open (about 15 minutes). Remove meat and discard shells. Combine shucked oysters or mussels with remaining ingredients.

Place in large container and cover. Let cool to room temperature, then chill in refrigerator at least 24 hours before serving.

In 1853, Mrs. J. Chadwick of Boston wrote *Home Cookery*, prescribing the addition of oysters in everything from bean soup to gumbo. Oyster wagons from Chesapeake Bay rolled through the streets of Boston and other New England towns. "Oyster Houses" in coastal cities offered oysters stewed, spiced, fried, baked, grilled, pickled and fricasseed.

Clam Balls

1 cup chopped clams,
    well drained
6 medium potatoes,
    baked and scooped
    out of the skin
2 eggs
2 tablespoons low-fat
    buttermilk
2 teaspoons grated onions
1 teaspoon Dijon mustard
1 teaspoon tarragon
salt and pepper to taste
skim milk for dipping
flour for dipping
$^1/_4$ cup canola oil for
    frying

SERVES 6

Wash clam meat. Rice or mash potatoes, then mix with chopped clams. One at a time, beat in eggs, then blend in buttermilk, onions and spices. Roll into 1-inch balls. Spray frying pan with non-stick oil. Pour in canola oil, heat on medium-high 7 minutes.

Dip clam balls in milk, then roll in flour. Fry until light brown. Serve with toothpicks and Tartare Sauce.

Classic Tartare Sauce

1 cup non-fat mayonnaise, 1 teaspoon mustard, 1 tablespoon parlsey, 1 tablespoon pickle relish, 2 teaspoons lemon juice, 1 teaspoon finely minced shallots, 1 tablespoon chopped capers, salt and pepper to taste.

COASTAL NEW ENGLAND   WINTERFARE COOKING

Black-Eyed Pea Caviar

SERVES 6-8

15-16 oz. can black-
    eyed peas, drained
15-16 oz. can white
    hominy, drained
2 medium tomatoes
4 green onions
1 large clove garlic
1 pepper, any color
$1/_4$ cup chopped cilantro
2 tablespoons parsley
1 cup picante sauce
    (mild, medium or hot)

Serving Suggestions:
baked tortilla chips
crackers
vegetable dippers

Combine black-eyed peas and hominy in a mixing bowl. Slice tomatoes in half, remove seeds, then chop into small pieces. Using just the white and green tender bases of the green onion, slice into small thin slivers. Crush garlic clove. Dice pepper. Combine all ingredients with black-eyed peas and hominy. Mix well and serve cold.

COASTAL NEW ENGLAND   WINTERFARE COOKING

Baked-Stuffed Mushroom Caps

1 lb. large cap mushrooms
1 cup plain bread crumbs
1 teaspoon rosemary,
    oregano or basil
pinch of pepper
pinch of salt
1 tablespoon safflower
    oil
2 tablespoons red or white
    wine
1 clove crushed garlic
2 tablespoons chopped
    scallions
paprika for tops

SERVES 4

Preheat oven to 350°. Spray large baking dish with non-stick oil.

Gently pop stems out of mushroom caps. Chop stems into small pieces, combine with bread crumbs and spices. Mix well.

Heat oil and wine in a small pan, add garlic and scallion. Sauté 2 minutes, then pour into stuffing mixture. Use a fork to distribute moisture. With a small teaspoon, press stuffing into mushroom caps. Place in baking pan, sprinkle tops with paprika. Bake 15 minutes, or until lightly browned on top.

The native tribes who inhabited the New England region used wild mushrooms, fungi, berries, flowers and plants for medicine and cooking. These included blue and yellow flag iris, truffles, purple loosestrife, turtlehead, American ginger, May apple, snakeroot, white yarrow, alfalfa, blackberries, Indian tobacco and tansy.

COASTAL NEW ENGLAND   WINTERFARE COOKING

Peppy Pimento Cutter Sandwiches

8 oz. non-fat cream
   cheese
4 oz. jar diced pimentos
8 drops Tabasco sauce
$1/_2$ teaspoon lime juice
pinch of garlic powder
pinch of pepper
pinch of salt
sliced white bread

SERVES 4

Allow cream cheese to soften at room temperature, then place in small mixing bowl. Drain diced pimentos and add to cream cheese with Tabasco sauce, lime juice and spices. Using a fork, blend well. Adjust seasonings to taste.

Trim crust from bread. With a rolling pin, lightly roll bread slices, compacting to half their original thickness. Spread pimento mixture on a slice, and cover with another slice of rolled bread. Cut each sandwich into 4 small squares.

COASTAL NEW ENGLAND   WINTERFARE COOKING

Rose Salmon Dip

15-16 oz. canned or fresh
    cooked salmon
$1/_3$ cup non-fat cottage
    cheese
3 canned artichoke hearts
1 scallion, chopped
4 drops Tabasco sauce
1 teaspoon Dijon mustard
1 tablespoon lemon juice
1 tablespoon dill
3 tablespoons pimento

MAKES $1^1/_2$ CUPS

Remove bones from canned salmon. Place in blender or food processor with remaining ingredients. Blend until smooth. Serve with French bread, bagels, or crackers.

Wickford Cove
Wickford, Rhode Island

COASTAL NEW ENGLAND   WINTERFARE COOKING

Zesty Spinach Dip

1 bag frozen chopped
   spinach
1 cup non-fat plain
   yogurt
1 cup non-fat cottage
   cheese
2 teaspoons lemon juice
4 drops Tabasco sauce
2 cloves minced garlic
2 tablespoons dill
1 teaspoon black pepper
1 teaspoon salt

MAKES $2^1/_2$ CUPS

In a fine sieve, defrost, drain and press moisture from chopped spinach.

Combine yogurt and cottage cheese in a blender. Process until smooth. Add lemon juice, Tabasco, garlic and spices. Process in blender again. Pour into bowl and mix in spinach. Cover and chill in refrigerator.

COASTAL NEW ENGLAND   WINTERFARE COOKING

Bill's Elegant Artichoke Dip

Serve with plain or cheese rice crackers for an exquisite sensory experience.

13-14 oz. can artichoke
hearts in water
4 oz. non-fat cream
cheese, softened at
room temperature
$^1/_2$ cup low-fat
mayonnaise
$^3/_4$ cup grated Parmesan
cheese

SERVES 4

Preheat oven to 350°. Spray small baking dish with non-stick oil.

Drain artichokes and chop into small pieces. In a small mixing bowl, blend together cream cheese,   mayonnaise and Parmesan cheese. Mix in artichoke hearts. Bake 20-25 minutes in prepared dish. Serve hot with crackers.

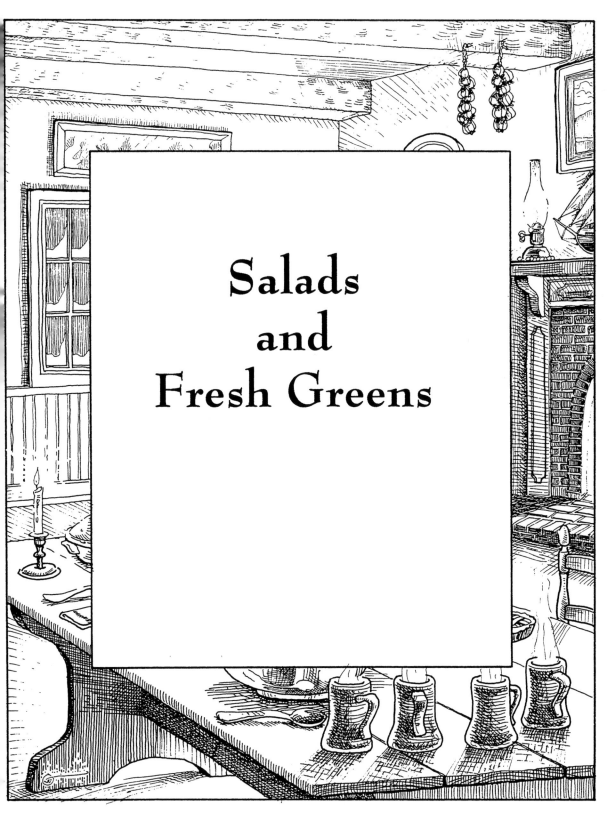

Salads
and
Fresh Greens

CONTENTS

COASTAL NEW ENGLAND   WINTERFARE COOKING

Hot Slaw with Sunflower Seeds

If you've been drying out last season's sunflowers, the seeds should be ready to use in this fresh hot slaw.

$^1/_2$ cup hulled sunflower
    seeds

SERVES 4

1 egg
2 tablespoons sugar
2 tablespoons vinegar
$^1/_2$ cup apple cider
1 teaspoon tamari or
    soy sauce
pinch of pepper
4 cups grated green
    cabbage

Lightly toast sunflower seeds on ungreased cookie sheet in 300° oven.

In a large saucepan, whisk together egg, sugar, vinegar, apple cider, tamari or soy sauce and pepper. Stirring constantly, cook over medium-low heat until thickened. Stir in cabbage, cover pan. Cook just until cabbage is hot and beginning to wilt. Place in serving bowl and sprinkle with toasted sunflower seeds. Serve hot.

COASTAL NEW ENGLAND   WINTERFARE COOKING

Sweet & Sour Kidney Bean Salad

2 cups dried kidney beans
4 tablespoons ketchup
3 tablespoons orange juice
3 tablespoons olive oil
2 tablespoons vinegar
2 teaspoons lemon juice
1 tablespoon dry mustard
3 tablespoons brown
   sugar
1 teaspoon garlic
2 tablespoons finely
   chopped sweet onions
   (Vidalia, red, purple)
1 tablespoon black pepper
2 tablespoons fresh
   parsley

SERVES 9

Soak kidney beans overnight. In the morning, rinse in cold water. Add beans to large pot of boiling water, cover and simmer until tender. Drain and chill.

Combine remaining ingredients together. Mix into chilled beans. Serve cold.

The broad harbors and protected bays of coastal New England helped the Yankees to establish a maritime economy. Tall timber forests provided lumber for shipbuilding and tall masts. The first vessel was launched into the Kennebec River in 1607, the 30-ton pinnace, *Virginia*. By 1700, shipbuilding had become a major industry.

COASTAL NEW ENGLAND   WINTERFARE COOKING

Eggplant Salad
A surprisingly good way to serve eggplant.

1 medium-sized eggplant
2 tomatoes
1 red pepper, chopped
    fine
1 small onion, grated
1 clove garlic, minced
1 teaspoon savory
pinch of salt
pinch of black pepper
3 tablespoons wine
    vinegar
2 tablespoons olive oil
1 tablespoon parsley

SERVES 4

Preheat broiler. Place eggplant on middle rack of oven, and turn it often to broil evenly on all sides. When the skin is blackened, remove eggplant and cool. Rub the skin off with a damp paper towel, and discard. Chop eggplant into small pieces.

Chop tomatoes into fine pieces, discarding excess seeds. Combine tomato with eggplant, pepper, onion and garlic.

In a small bowl, mix remaining ingredients. Pour over eggplant, toss and chill.

COASTAL NEW ENGLAND   WINTERFARE COOKING

Vegie Medley Pasta Salad

2 pkgs. fresh, refrigerated
    fettucine
1 green pepper
1 red pepper
1 head cauliflower
3 medium-sized carrots
4 radishes
12 mushrooms
1 small Vidalia, red or
    purple onion
$^3/_4$ cup wine vinegar
$^1/_2$ cup safflower oil
1 tablespoon sugar
2 teaspoons oregano
2 teaspoons basil
1 teaspoon tarragon
1 teaspoon black pepper

SERVES 6

Cook and drain fettucine. Place in a large bowl, cover and chill.

Cut peppers into slices. Chop cauliflower into florets. Peel and slice carrots. Slice radishes into rounds. Cut mushrooms into quarters. Chop onion. Put vegetables into a pot of boiling water and blanch 5 to 6 minutes. Pour vegetables into colander and then plunge into ice water. When chilled, drain.

Mix remaining ingredients to make dressing. Toss fettucine with vegetables and dressing. Chill before serving.

COASTAL NEW ENGLAND   WINTERFARE COOKING

Sweet & Sour Beets

3 cups cooked or canned
    beets, peeled and
    sliced
$^1/_2$ cup beet juice reserved
    from cooking or can
$^1/_2$ cup herbed vinegar
3 tablespoons sugar
pinch of salt
1 small onion, peeled and
    stuck with 3 cloves
1 teaspoon white pepper
$^1/_2$ bay leaf
$^1/_2$ teaspoon prepared
    horseradish

SERVES 6

Place sliced beets in a large glass jar.

Boil beet juice with vinegar, then add remaining ingredients. Bring back to a boil, and simmer 10 minutes. Pour into beet jar. When cool, cover jar and refrigerate. Chill at least 12 hours before serving.

Hearts of Palm
with Romaine Lettuce

2 cans hearts of palm
1 head romaine lettuce
1 red pepper
4 teaspoons chopped
    parsley
4 pinches paprika

Serve with either:
Herbed Italian
    Vinaigrette, page 63
Parmesan Dressing,
    page 64

SERVES 4

Drain hearts of palm, and cut into lengthwise strips. Arrange romaine on 4 salad plates, and place hearts of palm over romaine.

Slice red pepper into strips, arrange on plates. Sprinkle 1 teaspoon parsley and a pinch of paprika on each salad.

Serve with your choice of dressing.

COASTAL NEW ENGLAND   WINTERFARE COOKING

Hot Endive Salad

The tender white Belgian endives are grown without light. They can be home-grown in basements, or purchased fresh in the store year-round.

1 cup vegetable bouillon
    broth
8 Belgian endives

Serve with either:
Light Russian Dressing,
    page 64
Sweet Marjoram Italian
    Dressing, below

SERVES 4

Wash endives well, taking care to get out the grit between leaves. Briefly steam endives in broth until tender.

Cut off end of endives. Decoratively spread leaves of 2 endives on each salad plate. Serve while hot with dressing swirled over leaves.

Sweet Marjoram Dressing: This is an old-style herbal recipe with lots of flavor. Combine: $^1/_2$ cup olive oil; $^1/_2$ cup cider vinegar; 2 teaspoons dried sweet marjoram; $^1/_2$ teaspoon garlic powder, $^1/_2$ teaspoon Italian parsley, $^1/_2$ teaspoon paprika, salt and pepper to taste. Shake well. Refrigerate at least 3 hours.

COASTAL NEW ENGLAND   WINTERFARE COOKING

Arugula and Grapefruit Salad

Dressing:

$^1/_2$ cup unsweetened
   grapefruit juice
2 tablespoons Dijon
   mustard
3 tablespoons olive oil
1 teaspoon lemon juice
3 tablespoons honey
2 tablespoons poppy seeds
2 tablespoons finely
   grated onion
1 teaspoon black pepper
pinch of salt

4 packed cups torn
   arugula leaves
1 cup grapefruit sections

SERVES 4

In a small bowl, whisk together all dressing ingredients. Cover, and chill at least 2 hours to allow flavors to blend.

Just before serving, prepare and combine arugula leaves and grapefruit sections. Toss together with desired amount of salad dressing. (Note: this recipe makes extra dressing.)

COASTAL NEW ENGLAND   WINTERFARE COOKING

Artichoke and Pimento Salad

This recipe is my mother's fabulous "might-as-well-make it-a-meal" salad. Everyone eats so much of it, there's no room left for anything else!

2 13-oz. cans artichoke
    hearts
$1/_2$ cup thinly sliced
    pimento from canned
    whole pimentos
6 cups chopped lettuce
$1/_2$ cup grated Parmesan
    cheese
$1/_2$ cup olive oil
$1/_2$ cup red wine vinegar
2 cloves garlic, finely
    minced
2 tablespoons parsley
1 teaspoon sugar
salt and pepper to taste

SERVES 8

Chill all ingredients before starting. Drain artichokes and chop into bite-sized pieces. Combine in salad bowl with sliced pimento, lettuce and Parmesan cheese. Toss with remaining ingredients, and adjust seasonings and vinegar to taste. Serve at once.

Nauset Light, Eastham, Massachusetts

Chilled Lobster Salad

2 cups cooked lobster
    meat, cut into bite-
    sized pieces
$^3/_4$ cup non-fat
    mayonnaise
1 tablespoon lemon juice
1 shallot, minced
2 tablespoons sweet relish
1 teaspoon chervil
1 teaspoon parsley
salt and pepper to taste
1 tablespoon capers

SERVES 4

Place lobster meat in refrigerator to chill.

Whip together remaining ingredients. Fold into lobster meat. Chill thoroughly before serving.

Lobsters move about by darting backwards, using their abdomen and tail. Their shell is an external skeleton and is shed in the summer to grow a new one. Lobsters eat snails, clams, mussels, dead fish and even each other! Their large claw is used to crack shellfish, and the smaller claw for feeding. Deepwater lobsters weigh up to 40 pounds.

COASTAL NEW ENGLAND   WINTERFARE COOKING

Basil Tomato Aspic

4 cups chopped canned
    tomatoes and juice
2 tablespoons lemon juice
1 teaspoon sugar
1 teaspoon paprika
1 tablespoon basil
1 bay leaf
2 tablespoons chopped
    onion
$^1/_2$ teaspoon celery salt
$^1/_2$ teaspoon white pepper
2 tablespoons gelatin
$^1/_2$ cup cold water

Garnish:
watercress

SERVES 6

Simmer chopped tomatoes with their juice, lemon juice, sugar, paprika, basil, bay leaf, onion, celery salt and pepper for 30 minutes.

Soak gelatin in cold water. Stir into hot tomato mixture until gelatin has dissolved. Allow to thicken at room temperature.

Pour into wet mold. Chill until firm.

To unmold: Briefly set lower part of mold in warm water. Turn onto platter lined with watercress.

COASTAL NEW ENGLAND   WINTERFARE COOKING

Billie's Congealed Salad

For a pot-luck bash of Blue Hill's Bagaduce Chorale, the consensus was to give Billie (a good-cookin' southern woman) some slack for this salad's name.

1 pkg. lemon gelatin
1 pkg. lime gelatin
1 cup boiling water
1 can skimmed
    evaporated milk
1 cup non-fat mayonnaise
1 cup canned crushed
    pineapple, drained
1 cup non-fat cottage
    cheese

Optional:
$1/_3$ cup chopped pecans
$1/_3$ cup Maraschino
    cherries, drained

SERVES 8

In a large bowl, pour boiling water over gelatins. Mix until dissolved. Add milk and mayonnaise and beat with whisk until smooth. Press moisture out of pineapple, then stir into gelatin with cottage cheese. If desired, add pecans and/or Maraschino cherries.

Pour gelatin into wet mold. Refrigerate until firm, preferably overnight. Unmold onto platter.

COASTAL NEW ENGLAND   WINTERFARE COOKING

Herbed Italian Vinaigrette

$^1/_2$ cup white wine vinegar
3 cloves garlic, sliced
1 teaspoon oregano
1 teaspoon basil
1 teaspoon dill
$^1/_2$ cup vegetable broth
$^1/_3$ cup olive oil
1 tablespoon lemon juice
1 tablespoon grated
    Parmesan cheese
$^1/_2$ teaspoon pepper

MAKES 1$^1/_4$ CUPS

Simmer vinegar in uncovered stainless-steel pot with garlic, oregano, basil, dill and broth for 15 minutes. Transfer into blender and add olive oil, lemon juice, Parmesan and pepper. Process about 1 minute. Chill well.

Curried Dijon Salad Sauce

2 teaspoons gelatin
2 tablespoons cold water
1 cup vegetable broth
1 teaspoon sugar
1 tablespoon lemon juice
1 tablespoon curry powder
$^1/_4$ cup Dijon mustard

MAKES 1$^1/_3$ CUPS

Soak gelatin in cold water. Boil vegetable broth and add to gelatin mixture. Stir in remaining ingredients. Chill. Before serving dressing, beat with a wire whisk.

Parmesan Dressing

$^1/_2$ cup low-fat buttermilk
$^1/_2$ cup non-fat sour cream
2 tablespoons white wine
    vinegar
$^1/_3$ cup grated Parmesan
    cheese
1 teaspoon garlic, minced
2 teaspoons white pepper

MAKES $1^1/_8$ CUPS

Whisk all ingredients together until well blended. Chill before serving.

Thousand Island Dressing

$^1/_2$ cup non-fat plain yogurt
$^1/_2$ cup non-fat mayonnaise
$^1/_2$ cup non-fat cottage
    cheese
1 clove garlic, minced
1 teaspoon pepper
$^1/_3$ cup chili sauce
$^1/_4$ cup lemon juice
$^1/_4$ cup pickle relish

MAKES $2^1/_4$ CUPS

Combine yogurt, mayonnaise, cottage cheese, garlic and pepper in blender. Process until smooth. Transfer into bowl and whisk in remaining ingredients. Chill.

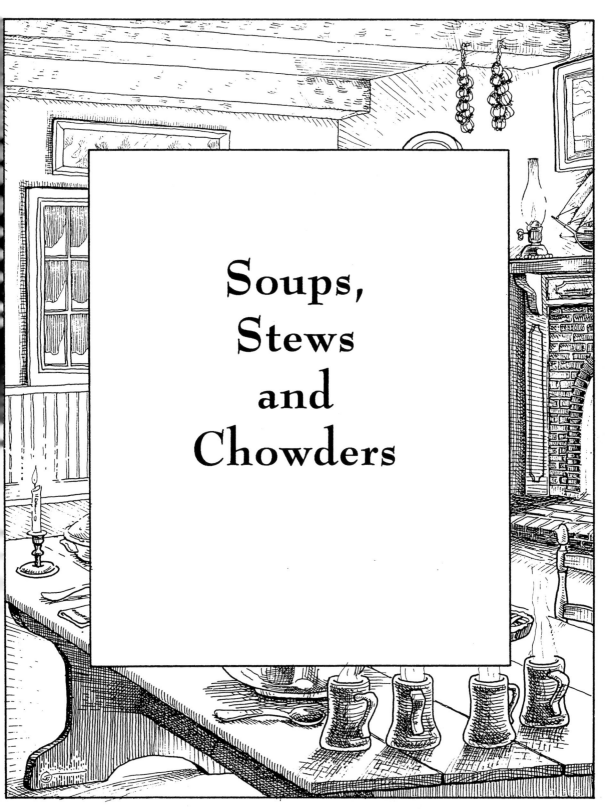

Soups, Stews and Chowders

COASTAL NEW ENGLAND   WINTERFARE COOKING

CONTENTS

COASTAL NEW ENGLAND   WINTERFARE COOKING

Freeport Shrimp Étouffé

1 tablespoon safflower oil
1 cup chopped yellow
    onion
1 cup chopped green
    pepper
2 cloves garlic, minced
4 stewed plum tomatoes
1 cup vegetable bouillon
    broth
1 cup tomato juice
1 teaspoon thyme
1 teaspoon saffron
1 bay leaf
$^1/_2$ teaspoon Tabasco
    sauce
1 cup white rice
2 lbs. small salad shrimp
3 tablespoons chopped
    parsley
$^1/_2$ cup skim milk

SERVES 4

In a large skillet, heat oil, sauté onion, pepper and garlic. Add bouillon broth, tomato juice, thyme, saffron, bay leaf and Tabasco sauce. Cover, simmer 10 minutes.

Mix in dry white rice. Chop salad shrimp into small pieces, and stir in. Simmer 25 minutes. Remove from heat, and add milk. Let set 10 minutes. Stir, then serve immediately.

Curried Butternut Soup

1 tablespoon sweet butter
2 tablespoons sherry or
    vermouth
2 cups chopped yellow
    onions
2 large butternut squash
2 tablespoons curry
1 teaspoon nutmeg
3 cups vegetable bouillon
    broth
1 cup apple juice
2 McIntosh apples,
    peeled and grated
salt and pepper to taste

Serve with:
non-fat sour cream

SERVES 6

In a large pot, melt butter with sherry or vermouth over low heat. Add chopped onions, cover and cook until clear, about 20 minutes.

Peel squash, remove seeds and cut into 1-inch cubes. Add squash and remaining ingredients to pot. Simmer 25 minutes.

Strain soup. Put solids into blender with 2 cups strained liquid. Process until smooth. Return to pot and mix in additional strained liquid until soup is of desired consistency. Heat 10 minutes. Serve with sour cream.

COASTAL NEW ENGLAND   WINTERFARE COOKING

Clear Mushroom Soup

4 cups vegetable bouillon
    broth
1 lb. mushrooms
$\frac{1}{4}$ cup sherry
parsley

SERVES 4

Bring bouillon broth to a boil. Wash and slice mushrooms to show their shape. Add mushrooms and sherry to bouillon and simmer 15 minutes. Clear Mushroom Soup may be served hot or cold. Garnish with parsley.

COASTAL NEW ENGLAND   WINTERFARE COOKING

Creamy Corn Clam Chowder

12 large quahog clams or
    36 littlenecks
2 cups boiling water
1 medium-sized onion,
    chopped fine
1 teaspoon butter
2 cups peeled and diced
    potatoes
1 teaspoon salt
1 teaspoon black pepper
3 cups skim milk blended
    with 1 cup non-fat
    powdered milk
1 tablespoon flour
1 cup pre-cooked corn
    kernels

SERVES 4

Scrub clams, discarding any that do not close. Steam clams in boiling water. Strain clam juice through very fine sieve and reserve.

Sauté onion in butter. Add potatoes, spices, milk and 1 cup reserved clam juice. Cover and simmer until potatoes are tender. Tranfer cooked mixture to blender. With blender running, add flour and process until smooth. Pour back into pot and cook 5 minutes.

Shuck clams and coarsely chop meat. Add clams and corn to chowder and cook 3 minutes more.

Soft-shell clams are mostly found north of Cape Cod, and are commonly called steamers. Hard-shell clams include the quahogs and littleneck clams, which are the most popular clams in New England. Wash clams several times to rinse out all the sand. Whether in the shell or shucked, clams should be plump and fresh-smelling.

COASTAL NEW ENGLAND   WINTERFARE COOKING

Lazyman's Lobster Stew

cooked meat of 2 lobsters
    cut into bite-sized
    pieces, about 2 cups
2 teaspoons butter
1 cup vermouth
3 cups skim milk blended
    with $1^1/_2$ cups non-fat
    powdered milk
1 teaspoon salt
1 teaspoon pepper

SERVES 4

Sauté lobster meat in butter. Add vermouth and simmer 5 minutes. Stir in remaining ingredients and heat, but do not boil.

COASTAL NEW ENGLAND   WINTERFARE COOKING

Nantucket Seafood Chowder

A medley of favorite seafood, Nantucket Seafood Chowder
makes a warming meal on a wintery day.

2 teaspoons butter
1 cup chopped onion
2 cups clam juice
2 cups potatoes,
    peeled and diced
1 cup sea scallops
1 lb. flounder fillets
1 cup lobster meat
2 cups skim milk
$1/2$ cup skimmed
    evaporated milk
1 tablespoon parsley
pinch of nutmeg
salt and pepper to taste

SERVES 6

In a large pot, sauté onion in butter until clear. Add clam juice and potatoes. Simmer until potatoes are tender.

Cut sea scallops and flounder into bite-sized pieces. Add scallops, flounder and lobster meat to pot. Simmer 10 minutes.

Reduce heat and add remaining ingredients. Heat well, but do not boil.

COASTAL NEW ENGLAND   WINTERFARE COOKING

Cheddar Chowder

SERVES 4

$^1/_2$ cup chopped onion
$^1/_2$ cup chopped celery
$^1/_2$ cup chopped carrots
1 tablespoon safflower oil
1 tablespoon sherry
$^1/_4$ cup flour
1 teaspoon paprika
1 teaspoon white pepper
2 cups vegetable bouillon
    broth
2 cups skim milk blended
    with 1 cup non-fat
    powdered milk
$^3/_4$ cup grated low-fat
    Cheddar cheese
1 tablespoon parsley

Cook onion, celery and carrots in oil until tender, but not brown. Blend in sherry, flour, paprika and pepper. Whisk in bouillon broth and milk.

Stirring constantly, cook over medium heat until thick and bubbly. Slowly stir in grated cheese and parsley.

COASTAL NEW ENGLAND   WINTERFARE COOKING

Stamford Crab Bisque

1 lb. cooked crab meat
3 tablespoons grated
    onion
1 clove garlic, halved
$^1/_2$ cup sliced mushrooms
3 cups skim milk
1 cup clam juice
1 tablespoon butter
3 tablespoons flour
$^1/_2$ teaspoon white pepper
pinch of mace
pinch of salt

SERVES 6

Pick through crab meat to be sure all shell pieces have been removed.

Simmer onion, garlic and mushrooms in milk and clam juice for 25 minutes, stirring frequently.

Heat butter in a saucepan, blend in flour to make a roux. Strain milk into roux, discarding vegetables. Whisk bisque until thick and smooth. Stir in white pepper, mace and salt. Gently fold crab meat into bisque. Heat, but do not boil.

In 1640, the Siwanoys Indians sold the land, now called Stamford, to the New Haven Colony. A settlement was begun there the following year. Located on a wide bay crossed by two tidal inlets, Stamford is home to the Bartlett Arboretum, a branch of the Whitney Museum of Art, and a 30,000 square-foot store of New England antiques.

COASTAL NEW ENGLAND   WINTERFARE COOKING

Creamy Potato Leek Soup

8 medium-sized potatoes
3 leeks, white stalks only
5 cups water
salt and pepper to taste
skim milk, optional

SERVES 4

Peel and quarter potatoes. Wash leeks thoroughly and cut stalks into 1-inch rounds. Place potatoes, leeks and water in covered pot. Simmer until vegetables are tender. Process potatoes, leeks and their water through food mill (or food processor, but texture will be bland). Stir in salt and pepper. If desired, thin with a little milk. Warm briefly over low heat before serving.

COASTAL NEW ENGLAND   WINTERFARE COOKING

Squash & Lentil Soup

2 cups red lentils
6 cups vegetable bouillon
     broth
1 cup white wine
1 cup chopped onion
1 cup peeled and diced
     carrots
1 cup diced celery
1 teaspoon thyme
2 teaspoons lemon juice
1 bay leaf
2 cups peeled acorn
     squash, diced into
     1-inch cubes
salt and pepper to taste

SERVES 6

Rinse lentils in cold water. Combine all ingredients, except squash, in a large covered pot. Stirring occasionally, simmer 1 hour, adding water if needed. Add squash and simmer another hour. Discard bay leaf. Adjust seasonings to taste.

COASTAL NEW ENGLAND   WINTERFARE COOKING

Rosemary Minestrone

Rosemary Minestrone is outstanding served with Parmesan or pesto.

1 cup small white beans
2 tablespoons olive oil
1 cup thin onion slivers
2 cloves garlic, minced
2 cups vegetable broth
6 cups water
2 cups grated cabbage
2 cups diced potatoes
1 cup chopped celery
2 cups diced zucchini
1 cup cut frozen green
    beans
2 cups chopped stewed
    plum tomatoes
2 tablespoons grated
    lemon rind
1 cup dry spaghetti,
    broken into pieces
2 teaspoons pepper
1 teaspoon salt
2 tablespoons rosemary
$1/4$ cup chopped parsley

SERVES 8

Wash and soak beans overnight in cold water. In the morning, rinse, and drain.

In a large pot, sauté onion and garlic in olive oil until soft, but not brown. Add beans, broth, water, cabbage, potatoes and celery. Bring to a boil, reduce heat and cover pot. Simmer 2 hours. Add remaining ingredients and cook another 30 minutes.

COASTAL NEW ENGLAND WINTERFARE COOKING

Cream of Cauliflower

5 medium-sized potatoes
1 medium-sized head of
    cauliflower
2 cups chopped yellow
    onions
4 cups water
salt and pepper to taste
skim milk, optional

SERVES 4

Peel and quarter potatoes. Cut cauliflower and stalks. Place potatoes, cauliflower, onion and water in covered pot. Simmer until very soft. Process vegetables and cooking water through food mill (or food processor, but texture will be bland). Stir in salt and pepper. If desired, thin with a little milk.

New Englanders get through winter "cabin-fever" by creating special events and attractions. The Mystic Valley Railway offers a Snowflake Special from Boston to the Berkshires, Boston also hosts the Sleigh Bell Parade and Reenactment of the Boston Tea Party. Mystic Seaport decorates in scenes of Christmas' past.

COASTAL NEW ENGLAND   WINTERFARE COOKING

Ratatouille Stew

2 cups peeled and diced
   eggplant
1 teaspoon salt
1 tablespoon olive oil
2 cloves garlic, minced
1 cup thinly sliced onion
1/2 cup thinly sliced red or
   green pepper
2 cups chopped stewed
   plum tomatoes and
   their juice
1 teaspoon brown sugar
1 cup vegetable broth
2 cups chopped zucchini
2 teaspoons oregano
1 tablespoon lemon juice
2 tablespoons basil
3 tablespoons parsley
2 teaspoons pepper

Optional:
non-fat sour-cream

SERVES 6

Toss eggplant with salt to remove excess moisture, and put in collander to drain over bowl.

Heat olive oil. Sauté eggplant with garlic, onion and peppers. Stir in tomatoes and juice, brown sugar, vegetable broth, zucchini, oregano, lemon juice, basil, parsley and pepper. Simmer 10 minutes.

Add drained liquid from eggplant to stew. Cover pot, simmer over medium heat 30 minutes. Uncover pot and simmer 30 minutes more. Adjust seasonings to taste.

If desired, serve with sour cream.

Matelote Stew

This celebration of freshwater fish originated in the Mediterranean region, and was adapted to suit the freshwater fish of New England.

12 small pearl onions
$^1/_2$ lb. mushrooms
$^1/_2$ lb. small salad shrimp,
   peeled
2 teaspoons olive oil
2 lbs. freshwater fish,
   ie. perch, trout, carp
3 cups red wine
3 cups fish stock or broth
1 tablespoon parsley
$^1/_2$ cup chopped celery
1 bay leaf
2 cloves garlic
1 teaspoon thyme
1 teaspoon salt
1 teaspoon pepper
2 tablespoons warm
   brandy
1 tablespoon butter
1 tablespoon olive oil
2 tablespoons flour

SERVES 6

Peel and cut pearl onions in half. Slice mushrooms. Wash shrimp. Sauté onions, mushrooms and shrimp in oil over low heat. Prepare the soup while these items steam together to make the garnish.

Clean and cut freshwater fish into bite-sized pieces. Place in pot with red wine and stock or broth. Add parsley, celery, bay leaf, garlic, thyme, salt and pepper. Bring to a boil, then reduce heat and simmer 5 minutes.
Remove pot from heat and float warm brandy on top. Ignite brandy. When flame burns out, return to stove, simmer 15 minutes. With a slotted spoon, transfer fish to oven dish, cover and keep warm. Make a roux of butter, olive oil and flour. Whisk into fish broth and heat to thicken, but do not boil. Put fish into soup bowls, cover with shrimp garnish, then ladle sauce on top.

Main Meal Dishes

CONTENTS

Any fish, cooked by any means, generally requires only 10 minutes of cooking time for each inch of thickness, measured at its thickest part.

COASTAL NEW ENGLAND   WINTERFARE COOKING

Oven-Fried Ipswich Clams

Ispwich clams come out of the Essex River in Massachusetts. If possible, use real Ipswich clams, famous for their lucious flavor and tenderness.

3 cups raw, shucked
    Ipswich or littleneck
    clams
1 tablespoon canola oil
2 egg whites
1 cup flour
1 teaspoon salt
1 teaspoon pepper
1 teaspoon paprika
1 teaspoon dried parsley

SERVES 4

Preheat oven to 400°. Spray a baking pan with 3 coats of non-stick oil. Pat dry the shucked clams in a towel.

In a small bowl, combine oil and egg whites together with about 15 strokes. In a separate bowl, mix flour and spices.

Dip clams in liquid mixture, then coat in herbed flour. Shake off extra flour in sieve, then place on wax paper until flour is absorbed by moisture.

Place clams in a single layer on prepared baking pan, set on lowest rack of oven. After 5 minutes, flip clams to brown on other side. Bake until browned and crispy. Serve hot.

COASTAL NEW ENGLAND WINTERFARE COOKING

Wicked Good
Lobster Feast

2 cups white wine
6 dozen steamer clams
6 lobsters, 1-1¹/₂ lbs. each
6 ears of corn, husked
12 very small red potatoes

Butter-Wine Sauce:
2 tablespoons hot melted
    butter
¹/₂ cup strained poaching
    wine from steamed
    lobster/clams
3 tablespoons lemon juice
salt and pepper to taste

SERVES 6

Pour wine into 24-quart steamer pot. Cover and heat until it steams.

Scrub clams, discarding any with broken shells or that do not close tightly when handled. Tie clams by the dozen, in squares of cheesecloth tied with string. Allow room in bags for clams to open.

Place potatoes in covered pot. 10 minutes later, add lobsters and corn. After 15 minutes, add steamer bags. Steam clams until they open, about 12 minutes. In a saucepan, combine ingredients for Butter-Wine Sauce, simmer 10 minutes. Serve in dipping bowls.

COASTAL NEW ENGLAND   WINTERFARE COOKING

How to Eat
Lobster and Clams

Lobster: Bend back claws and flippers and break off where attached to body. Use cracker and pick to crack claws and knuckles, and remove meat. Suck meat from small flippers.

Bend back tail and break off from body. Tail flippers can also be broken back and the meat pushed out, or you can cut the membrane. In the body is the green tomalley (liver) and the red coral of the females (roe).

Clams: Wedge open shells and loosen meat. Dip in broth to rinse off sand.

COASTAL NEW ENGLAND   WINTERFARE COOKING

Pan-Fried Tuna Steaks

4 tuna steaks, sized to
   suit appetites
$1/2$ cup flour
2 teaspoons paprika
2 teaspoons tarragon
2 teaspoons pepper
$1/2$ teaspoon salt
1 teaspoon garlic powder
2 egg whites
2 tablespoons olive oil

SERVES 4

Preheat frying pan on medium-high heat.

Combine flour and spices in a mixing bowl. In a separate bowl, whisk egg whites until frothy. Dip tuna steaks in egg whites, then in flour. Shake off excess flour and place on wax paper.

Spray hot frying pan with non-stick oil and coat pan with olive oil. When oil is hot, fry tuna steaks, nicely browning on each side. Check to see that inside of steaks are cooked (they should be opaque, not translucent.)

COASTAL NEW ENGLAND   WINTERFARE COOKING

Shrimp Kebabs in Beer Marinade

1$^1/_2$ lbs. medium-sized
   raw shrimp (41-50
   count) peeled and
   deveined
$^1/_2$ cup pre-cooked,
   canned pearl onions
12 cherry tomatoes
1 can beer, any kind
1 tablespoon parsley
1 tablespoon basil
1 teaspoon minced garlic
2 teaspoons dry mustard
1 tablespoon lemon juice
1 teaspoon pepper
$^1/_2$ teaspoon celery salt
3 cups cooked rice

SERVES 4

Clean, rinse and dry shrimp. Place shrimp, pearl onions and tomatoes in mixing bowl.

In a separate bowl, mix together remaining ingredients. Pour over shrimp and vegetables. Cover and chill until ready to broil.

Preheat broiler. Arrange shrimp, pearl onions and tomatoes on flat, double edged skewers. Rest ends of skewers on lips of baking pan, to catch the drippings. Place on rack nearest broiler, turn skewers and baste after 4 minutes. Broil 3-4 minutes on second side. Serve on bed of rice.

COASTAL NEW ENGLAND   WINTERFARE COOKING

Coquilles St. Jacques

1¹/₂ lbs. scallops, whole if
    small, quartered or
    halved if large
1 cup dry vermouth
1 bay leaf
1 tablespoon butter
2 tablespoons white wine
3 tablespoons flour
³/₄ cup skim milk blended
    with ¹/₄ cup non-fat
    powdered milk
¹/₂ teaspoon salt
1 teaspoon white pepper
¹/₂ teaspoon freshly
    squeezed lemon juice
¹/₄ cup grated low-fat
    Swiss Lorraine cheese

SERVES 4

Prepare scallops: Boil vermouth with bay leaf. Poach the scallops in the boiling liquid for 2 minutes, remove pot from heat but leave in hot liquid 10 minutes more. With a slotted spoon, transfer scallops to a bowl. Remove bay leaf, boil down poaching liquid to 1 cup.

In a saucepan, heat butter and white wine. Blend in flour, cook 1 minute. Remove from heat and whisk in milk, poaching liquid, salt and pepper. Simmer and stir over medium heat. If too thick, add a little milk.

Remove sauce from heat, stir in lemon juice. Fold into scallops and transfer to baking dish. Sprinkle with grated cheese. Just before serving, place 5-inches under broiler until bubbly and light brown.

COASTAL NEW ENGLAND   WINTERFARE COOKING

Smoked Trout Mousse

This mousse makes a cool showing at a holiday buffet or potluck.

2 cups part-skim Ricotta
   cheese
3 tablespoons prepared
   horseradish
1 tablespoon finely
   chopped green onions
2 tablespoons prepared
   sweet mustard
$1/2$ teaspoon salt
1 teaspoon black pepper
2 cups flaked smoked
   trout

Serve on:
salad greens with
   lemon slices

SERVES 6

In a food processor or blender, purée Ricotta until completely smooth. Transfer to mixing bowl and blend in horseradish, chopped green onion, mustard, salt and pepper. Fold in flaked trout and gently mix well.

Place mixture into wet 1-quart fish (or other-shaped) mold. Chill at least 6 hours before serving. Unmold trout mousse on a bed of greens decorated with lemon slices.

The potluck was borne of necessity (barn-raisings and other events requiring a community spirit always went best with food.) Potlucks today are also an easy way to gather friends and family for a meal, a holiday, or special celebration, and to share the offering of food. The only potluck rule is to bring plenty, especially if your cooking is good!

COASTAL NEW ENGLAND   WINTERFARE COOKING

Frenchman's Bay
Baked Stuffed Lobster

6 live lobsters, 1-1$^1/_2$ lbs.
2 teaspoons butter
3 tablespoons chopped
    shallots
2 cloves garlic, minced
$^1/_3$ cup sherry
1 tablespoon balsamic
    vinegar
1 tablespoon lemon juice
3 tablespoons parsley
1 teaspoon pepper
3 cups bread crumbs
2 tablespoons canola oil

SERVES 4

Steam lobsters in a large covered pot of 2-inches boiling water. Lobsters will be cooked in 20-25 minutes, depending on their size. Remove lobsters and reserve 2 cups of liquid. Remove the tail and claw meat from the two smallest lobsters and chop it into small pieces.

Heat butter in saucepan. Sauté shallots and garlic. Add sherry, vinegar, lemon juice, parsley and pepper. Stir in bread crumbs, then chopped lobster meat.

Split the other 4 lobsters down the underside of the body. Clean out the bodies, adding the green tomalley and red coral to the bread crumb mixture, if desired. Fill the lobster bodies with the stuffing. Brush shells with canola oil and place on baking sheet. Bake in preheated 400° oven 20 minutes.

COASTAL NEW ENGLAND   WINTERFARE COOKING

Simple Fillet of Sole Bon Femme

8 equal-sized fillets of
    sole
2 cups sliced mushrooms
1 cup white wine
1 teaspoon butter
$^3/_4$ cup skim milk blended
    with $^1/_4$ cup non-fat
    powdered milk
1 tablespoon flour
2 teaspoons tarragon
salt and pepper to taste
1 teaspoon lemon juice

SERVES 4

Preheat oven to 400°. Spray baking pan with non-stick oil.

Place 4 fillets in pan, cover with mushrooms, then place second fillet over mushrooms. Pour wine in pan. Poach in oven 15 minutes. Remove pan and drain juices into saucepan.

To cooking juice in saucepan, whisk in butter, milk, flour, tarragon, salt and pepper. Rapidly boil down until consistency of heavy cream. Remove from heat and stir in lemon juice. Spread sauce over fillets. Return to oven 6-7 minutes, to heat through.

COASTAL NEW ENGLAND   WINTERFARE COOKING

Fancy Flounder
with Piquant Tomato Sauce

2¹/₂ lbs. flounder fillets
1 cup white wine
1 cup chopped yellow
    onion
1 tablespoon olive oil
1 tablespoon lemon juice
1 teaspoon oregano
2 tablespoons tiny capers
1¹/₂ cups canned Italian
    plum tomatoes,
    finely chopped,
    with their juices
2 teaspoons butter

SERVES 6

Preheat oven to 350°. Place flounder in an oven dish and pour wine over fish. Poach in oven just until cooked through. Drain liquid and set aside. Cover fish to keep warm.

In a saucepan, sauté onion in olive oil. When onion is clear, add lemon juice, oregano, capers, tomatoes and juice. Rapidly boil down until sauce is very thick. Reduce heat.

Add poaching liquid to tomato sauce. Rapidly boil down until about 1¹/₂ cups remain. Stir in butter. Serve immediately with Piquant Tomato Sauce spooned over flounder.

To trim your Christmas tree New England style, string popcorn and cranberries into ropes. Tree trimmings might include a small bird's nest, toy sail boats, miniature lobster pots and buoys. An old quilt makes a lovely tree skirt. For an old-fashioned Christmas Eve, plan a lights-out party, with only candlelight and the lights of the tree shining.

COASTAL NEW ENGLAND   WINTERFARE COOKING

Cranberry Stuffed Rockport Haddock

$2^1/_2$ lbs. haddock fillets
1 tablespoon canola oil
$^1/_2$ cup chopped onion
1 tablespoon lemon juice
1 cup cleaned cranberries,
   fresh or frozen
$^1/_2$ cup brown sugar
$^1/_2$ cup orange juice
2 tablespoons parsley
2 cups cooked white or
   brown rice
1 egg, beaten
1 teaspoon canola oil
1 teaspoon paprika

SERVES 6

Spray a large casserole with non-stick oil. Place half the fillets on bottom of casserole.

Sauté onion in a tablespoon of oil. Add lemon juice, cranberries, brown sugar and orange juice. Simmer 25 minutes.

In a mixing bowl, combine cranberry sauce with parsley, cooked rice and beaten egg. Spread mixture over haddock fillets. Place remaining fillets over cranberry mixture. Brush fillets with oil, sprinkle with paprika.

Bake 35 minutes in preheated 350° oven.

COASTAL NEW ENGLAND   WINTERFARE COOKING

Codfish Balls

1 lb. salt codfish
3 cups fish bouillon broth
3 medium-sized potatoes,
    cut into quarters
2 teaspoons grated lemon
    rind
$^1/_4$ cup grated onion
$^1/_2$ cup pre-cooked corn
    kernels
pinch of cayenne
1 teaspoon pepper
1 egg
1 tablespoon skim milk
3 tablespoons flour
4 tablespoons safflower
    oil
prepared tartare or
    seafood sauce

SERVES 4

Soak salted codfish in cold water for 6 hours, rinsing and changing the water every hour.

Bring bouillon broth and potatoes to a boil. Simmer until potatoes are tender. Wrap desalted codfish in a cheesecloth and place in broth. Simmer 5 minutes, then remove pot from heat. Leave fish in hot broth another 5-10 minutes depending on thickness of fish. Remove codfish from cheesecloth and pat dry.

Put codfish in bowl and use two forks to flake into shreds. In a separate bowl, mash potatoes. Stir potatoes, lemon rind, onion, corn, cayenne, pepper, egg, milk and flour into codfish. Form into 1-inch balls.

Preheat and spray a frying pan with non-stick oil. Coat pan with safflower oil, and fry codfish balls until browned. Serve with tartare or seafood sauce.

COASTAL NEW ENGLAND   WINTERFARE COOKING

Salmon Croquettes

2 cups cooked salmon,
    fresh or canned
1 tablespoon lemon juice
1 medium potato, peeled,
    boiled and mashed
1 onion, grated
1 egg, beaten
1 teaspoon pepper
pinch of salt
$^1/_2$ cup all-purpose flour
3 tablespoons safflower
    oil

Serve with:
non-fat sour cream
    blended with lemon
    juice, salt and pepper

SERVES 4

Flake salmon apart, removing bones. In a mixing bowl, combine salmon with lemon juice, mashed potato, onion, beaten egg, spices and flour. Stir well. Form into 3-inch croquette patties, about $^1/_2$ inch thick.

Preheat frying pan. Spray with non-stick oil, then coat with safflower oil. Carefully place croquettes in hot oil. Fry until browned on both sides, then drain on paper towels. Serve hot with seasoned sour cream.

COASTAL NEW ENGLAND   WINTERFARE COOKING

Honey-Orange Glazed Salmon

Honey-Orange Glazed Salmon is a marvelous blend of flavors.

2 lbs. salmon fillets
$^1/_2$ cup orange juice
$^1/_2$ cup honey
1 teaspoon butter
1 tablespoon lemon juice
$^1/_2$ teaspoon pepper
pinch of salt

SERVES 4

Cut salmon into 4 portions. Check for bones, and remove any with pliers. Pat fish dry with paper towels.

In a small saucepan, combine remaining ingredients. Simmer sauce for 15 minutes.

Preheat broiler. Spray oven pan with non-stick oil. Place salmon on pan and coat with sauce. Slide under broiler on upper rack, leaving oven door tipped open. Baste with sauce every 5 minutes. When fillets start to brown on top, close oven door and fish will cook through in 3 minutes (do not flip fish). Spoon extra sauce over fish before serving.

COASTAL NEW ENGLAND   WINTERFARE COOKING

Broiled Swordfish Steaks

4 swordfish steaks, sized
   to suit appetites
2 tablespoons olive oil
2 tablespoons lemon juice
2 tablespoons tamari or
   soy sauce
1 teaspoon pepper

SERVES 4

Cut off any visible fat from swordfish steaks.

In a shallow pan, make a marinade of olive oil, lemon juice, tamari or soy sauce, and pepper. Soak swordfish steaks in marinade, spooning liquid over tops of steaks. Cover pan, and refrigerate at least 1 hour.

Preheat broiler. Spray broiler pan with non-stick oil (for easier clean-up). Place swordfish on upper oven rack under broiler, leaving oven door tipped open. When browned, turn steaks over, baste with marinade, and broil on second side.

Whale watching cruises in New England can be taken out of many ports. Humpback and finback whales are commonly seen, especially where there are banks and underwater mountain chains which breed plankton and krill for the whales to feed on. The New England whales winter and bear their young in the Caribbean, then migrate north.

Cacciucco

Squid is customarily used in Cacciucco. A local fisherman claims that they are twice as sweet as lobster and only half the trouble to fix.

¹/₂ lb. squid or lobster
    meat
¹/₂ lb. raw shrimp,
    peeled and deveined
2 tablespoons olive oil
2 cloves garlic, minced
1 small hot red pepper
¹/₂ cup white wine
2 teaspoons parsley
2 tablespoons oregano
1 tablespoon grated
    lemon rind
¹/₂ cup Madeira
2 tablespoons tomato
    paste
2¹/₂ cups water
pinch of salt
1 lb. cod fillets, skinned
¹/₂ lb. scallops
¹/₂ lb. halibut
6 slices Italian bread
1 clove garlic, cut in half

SERVES 6

Clean squid: Remove the spiny portion, which looks like a translucent rod. Pull the head and legs from the envelope-like covering. If desired, remove ink sac at the base of the head. Cut squid and shrimp into small pieces.

In a deep pot, heat oil, sauté garlic and whole hot pepper. Add squid and shrimp. Cover and cook 30 minutes. Add white wine and simmer, uncovered, until it evaporates.

Mix in parsley, oregano, lemon rind, Madeira, tomato paste, water and salt. Cut cod, scallops and halibut into pieces; add to stew. Cover and simmer 15 minutes. Add water if needed, but stew must be thick.

Toast bread, rub with cut garlic and place in bowls. Remove hot red pepper, adjust seasonings, and ladle stew over toast.

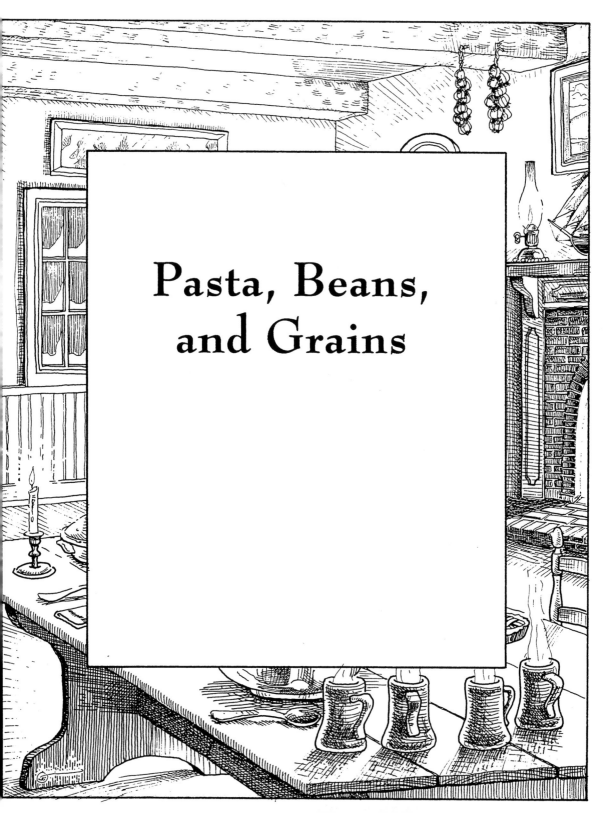

Pasta, Beans, and Grains

COASTAL NEW ENGLAND   WINTERFARE COOKING

CONTENTS

Any Pasta, Beans and Grains recipe can be used for a
main dish or side dish by varying the amount per person.

COASTAL NEW ENGLAND   WINTERFARE COOKING

Lobster Linguine

2 tablespoons olive oil
1 tablespoon butter
1 clove garlic, minced
1 teaspoon mace
1 teaspoon white pepper
3 tablespoons prepared
    sweet mustard sauce
$^1/_4$ cup clam juice
$^2/_3$ cup cognac
2 cups cooked lobster
    meat, cut into bite-
    sized pieces
2 pkgs. fresh, refrigerated
    linguine

SERVES 4

Set a large pot of water to boil.

Heat olive oil and butter in saucepan. Add garlic and sauté until clear. Stir in mace, pepper, mustard sauce, clam juice and cognac. Add lobster and heat 10 minutes.

Place pasta in boiling water. When tender, drain and place on dinner plates. With a slotted spoon, remove lobster from sauce. Toss pasta and sauce together to coat evenly. Place pasta on dinner plates, and lobster pieces on top.

101

Creamy Sea Shells
with Smoked Salmon

2 cups dry small pasta
shells
1 tablespoon canola oil
2 tablespoons flour
1 cup skim milk
1 teaspoon black pepper
2 teaspoons grated onion
$^1/_2$ cup grated low-fat
Cheddar cheese
$^1/_2$ cup non-fat sour cream
1 cup hot-smoked salmon
(not moist "lox"
strips), broken into
bite-sized pieces
1 teaspoon lemon juice

SERVES 4

Boil pasta until tender. Prepare sauce while pasta is cooking.

In a small saucepan, heat oil, then blend in flour. Slowly whisk in milk, then pepper and onion. Stirring constantly, allow sauce to thicken. Turn off heat, and while stirring, gradually add grated Cheddar until it is melted. Remove from heat and fold in sour cream and smoked salmon. Mix in lemon juice.

When pasta is cooked, drain and toss with sauce. Serve at once.

COASTAL NEW ENGLAND   WINTERFARE COOKING

Fisherman's Pot Pie

$2^1/_2$ cups all-purpose flour
$^1/_2$ cup safflower oil
6 tablespoons ice water
1 tablespoon skim milk
20 small pearl onions
$^1/_4$ cup chopped celery
1 tablespoon safflower oil
3 tablespoons flour
2 teaspoons thyme
1 cup vegetable broth
1 cup skim milk blended
    with $^1/_2$ cup non-fat
    powdered milk
1 cup frozen corn kernels
$1^1/_2$ cups raw fish, cut
    into bite-sized pieces
2 cups cleaned, raw
    shellfish (shrimp,
    clams, lobster...)
1 teaspoon skim milk

SERVES 6

Preheat oven to 400°. Spray a pie dish with non-stick oil.

Cut $^1/_2$ cup oil into flour with pastry cutter or knives, until mixture resembles texture of peas. Stir in ice water, then skim milk. Divide dough and roll between floured sheets of waxed paper to make top and bottom crusts for pie dish. Place bottom crust in pie dish.

Peel small onions and sauté them with celery in 1 tablespoon safflower oil. Stir in flour and thyme. Slowly whisk in vegetable broth and milk. Cook until thickened.

Add corn, fish and shellfish. Pour into pie dish, then cover with top crust. Pinch and flute edges together. Brush top with 1 teaspoon milk and make slits in top crust with knife. Bake 30 minutes.

Shells Stuffed with Crab Ricotta

$^1/_2$ lb. large pasta shells
    for stuffing
2 teaspoons safflower oil
2 cups part-skim Ricotta
    cheese
$^1/_2$ cup grated low-fat
    Swiss Lorraine cheese
1 lb. fresh or canned crab
    meat
2 teaspoons garlic powder
1 teaspoon white pepper
2 tablespoons parsley
$^1/_2$ cup chopped onion
$^1/_2$ cup chopped pepper
1 clove garlic, minced
2 teaspoons olive oil
2 cups chopped plum
    tomatoes and juice
$^1/_4$ cup tomato paste
1 bay leaf
1 teaspoon oregano
salt and pepper to taste

SERVES 6

Rapidly boil pasta shells in a large quantity of water until tender, but firm to the bite. Drain, return to pot and toss with safflower oil to keep them from sticking together.

In a mixing bowl, combine Ricotta, Swiss Lorraine, crab meat, garlic powder, white pepper and parsley. Stuff filling into shells and place in a large baking pan that's been sprayed with non-stick oil.

Sauté onion, pepper and garlic in olive oil. Add remaining ingredients and rapidly cook down until sauce has thickened. Remove bay leaf and spoon over stuffed shells. Bake in 350° oven for 30 minutes.

Fettucine Alfredo with Baby Peas & Blackened Scallops

2 lbs. sea scallops (about $^3/_4$-inch in diameter)
3 tablespoons paprika
1 tablespoon onion powder
2 teaspoons garlic powder
2 teaspoons cumin
1 teaspoon cayenne
1 tablespoon safflower oil
2 pkgs. fresh, refrigerated fettucine noodles
1 cup skim milk blended with $^1/_3$ cup non-fat powdered milk
$1^1/_2$ cups grated Parmesan
$1^1/_2$ cups frozen baby peas
1 teaspoon black pepper

SERVES 6

Toss scallops in a collander, and lightly pat dry on a cotton towel. In a small, sturdy paper bag, combine spices. Place half of the scallops in the paper bag and shake well. Pick out scallops, and shake the remaining scallops in the spice bag.

Heat a cast-iron frying pan on high heat. Briefly spray with non-stick oil, then brush with oil. Pan blacken scallops on both sides.

Boil noodles in a large quantity of water. Drain. Add milk and Parmesan a little at a time, tossing after each addition. Stir in scallops and peas. Heat, season with pepper.

Shrimp Creole

2 tablespoons canola oil
4 tablespoons flour
1$^1/_2$ cups vegetable
    bouillon broth
1 tablespoon canola oil
2 tablespoons dry sherry
$^3/_4$ cup chopped onion
$^3/_4$ cup chopped green
    pepper
1$^1/_2$ cups chopped stewed
    tomatoes and juice
1 bay leaf
1 teaspoon brown sugar
$^1/_2$ teaspoon cayenne
salt and pepper to taste
1 lb. frozen, pre-cooked
    and deveined shrimp,
    thawed and drained
3 cups cooked rice

SERVES 4

Heat 2 tablespoons oil in a large saucepan over low heat. Make a roux by blending in flour and brown. Whisk in vegetable broth, and cook over medium-low heat.

In a separate saucepan, sauté onion and green pepper in sherry and 1 tablespoon oil until browned. Stir in stewed tomatoes and their juice, bay leaf, brown sugar, cayenne, salt and pepper. Rapidly cook down over medium-high heat until liquid is reduced by half. Stir into flour roux, cook until thickened. Add shrimp and simmer for 5 minutes.

Serve over bed of hot rice.

COASTAL NEW ENGLAND   WINTERFARE COOKING

Rhode Island Risotto
with Parmesan Cheese

3 shallots, diced
2 tablespoons olive oil
$1/4$ cup grated carrot
1 clove garlic, minced
2 cups dry arborio rice
$1/2$ cup Marsala
1 tablespoon powdered
   vegetable stock or
   crushed bouillon cube
1 cup frozen peas, thawed
$1/2$ cup red pepper, diced
2 canned tomatoes,
   chopped and drained
1 tablespoon butter
1 teaspoon black pepper
$1/2$ cup fresh grated
   Parmesan cheese

SERVES 4 (8 AS A SIDE DISH)

In a large saucepan, sauté shallots in oil. Add carrot and garlic, cook until shallots are clear. Stir in rice, then turn heat to high and add Marsala. Cook until liquid is reduced by half. Reduce heat to medium.

In a separate pot, mix powdered stock or boullion into 6 cups boiling water. Add hot broth to risotto, $1/2$ cup at a time. Stir, and allow rice to absorb liquid after each addition. Some liquid will remain after final addition of broth. Add peas, pepper and tomato, cook 5 minutes, adding more liquid if needed. When rice is creamy and soft, stir in butter, pepper and Parmesan.

COASTAL NEW ENGLAND   WINTERFARE COOKING

Wild Rice Ring with Water Chestnuts

1 cup wild rice
4 cups water
1 teaspoon salt
1 tablespoon canola oil
$^1/_2$ cup chopped onion
1 clove garlic, minced
$^1/_2$ cup finely chopped
   celery
$^1/_2$ cup chopped
   mushrooms
$^1/_4$ cup sherry
1 teaspoon nutmeg
1 small can water
   chestnuts
1 tablespoon chopped
   parsley

SERVES 6

Wash wild rice several times, pouring off particles that float. Boil water and salt, then stir in rice. Cover and simmer 40 minutes or until tender. Do not stir while cooking.

Sauté onion, garlic, celery and mushrooms in oil. Turn off heat, add sherry and nutmeg. Combine with cooked rice. Press into 7-inch ring mold that has been sprayed with non-stick oil. Place ring mold in a pan of hot water in the oven. Bake at 350° for 20 minutes. Loosen edges and turn onto serving platter. Drain water chestnuts, toss with parsley, and place in center of ring.

Hulled Barley and Sesame Seeds

1 cup whole-grain hulled
    barley
3 cups water
$^1/_2$ teaspoon salt
3 tablespoons sesame
    seeds

SERVES 4

Boil barley in salted water until tender, about $1^1/_2$ hours.

Spread sesame seeds on cookie sheet and toast in 300° oven until light brown (they burn quickly so watch carefully).

When barley has absorbed all the water and is soft, transfer to serving dish. Sprinkle toasted sesame seeds on top, and serve hot.

Since wheat does not grow well in New England, rye, cornmeal, barley and buckwheat are the grains and flours of traditional local cooking. Barley and winter rye grow farther north than any other food plant. The early settlers also found these grains would grow when scattered in newly cleared soil, even before tree stumps could be cleared for plowing.

COASTAL NEW ENGLAND   WINTERFARE COOKING

Baked Beans

2 cups dried beans
   (any kind)
6 cups water
$1/3$ cup chopped onion
$1/4$ cup dark molasses
3 tablespoons ketchup
1 cup chopped canned
   tomatoes and juice
2 tablespoons canola oil
1 cup beer
2 teaspoons curry powder
1 tablespoon
   Worcestershire sauce

SERVES 6

Wash beans. Put in pot with water and bring to a full boil. Simmer 30 minutes, then remove from heat. Let sit 1 hour, then return to heat and simmer 1 hour, or until tender. Mix in all other ingredients.

Tranfer into covered bean pot. Bake in 250° oven 6 to 7 hours, adding water if necessary.

COASTAL NEW ENGLAND   WINTERFARE COOKING

Hopping John

Eat Hopping John on New Year's Day and you'll have good luck all year.

2 cups dried black-eyed
   peas
6 cups soup broth, any
   kind
2 cups chopped onions
1 teaspoon black pepper
1 teaspoon cayenne
2 cloves garlic, minced
3 bay leaves

Serve with:
boiled rice

SERVES 8

Wash dried black-eyed peas, then bring to a boil in broth. Simmer 5 mintues, then remove from heat and let stand 1 hour.

Add remaining ingredients to pot, and bring back to a boil. Simmer 2 hours. Remove bay leaves and slightly mash mixture.

Serve over hot boiled rice.

COASTAL NEW ENGLAND   WINTERFARE COOKING

Succotash

2 cups cooked lima beans
2 cups cooked corn
   (fresh or frozen)
1 tablespoon butter
1 teaspoon salt
1 teaspoon pepper
1 teaspoon paprika

Garnish:
parsley

SERVES 6

Boil water in bottom pan of double boiler. In the top pan, combine all ingredients. Cover and cook 30 minutes over boiling water.

Transfer to serving bowl and sprinkle with chopped parsley.

During the eighteenth century, Indian corn was the most important crop, and the food staple of settlers and Indians. The Indians had taught the settlers to plant corn "When the oakleaf is as big as a mouse's ear." The native women instructed them to poke a hole in the ground, drop in 4 or 5 corn kernels, and part of a dead fish for fertilizer.

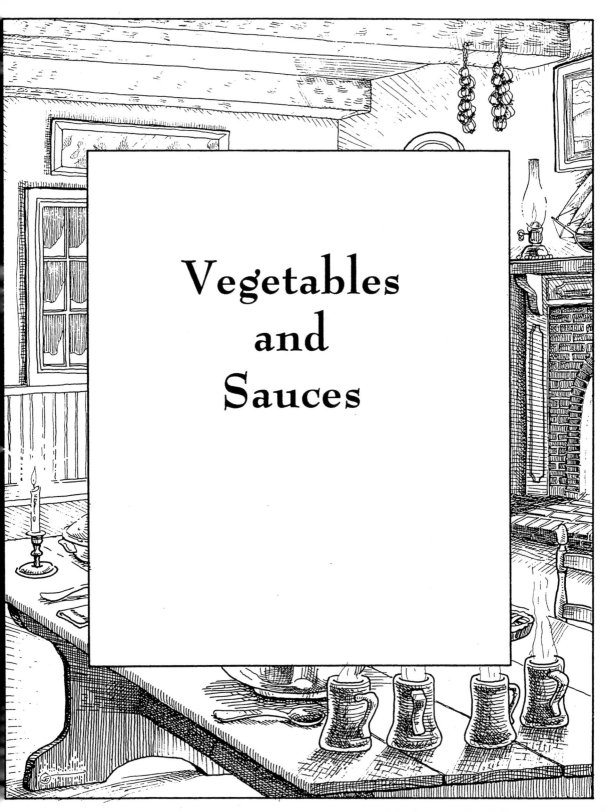

Vegetables
and
Sauces

CONTENTS

COASTAL NEW ENGLAND   WINTERFARE COOKING

Carrot Tzimmes

3 tablespoons barley
5 cups carrots, peeled
     and cut into 1-inch
     rounds
1 cup grated apple
pinch of salt
2 tablespoons honey
$^1/_2$ cup water
2 tablespoons canola oil
$^1/_2$ teaspoon powdered
     ginger

SERVES 6

Bring barley and 1 cup water to a boil in a covered pot. Turn off heat and let set 1 hour, then drain off water.

Add remaining ingredients, including $^1/_2$ cup of water, to the pot. Place on low heat, cover, and cook at least 1 hour, until barley is tender. Stir occasionally, and add more water if tzimmes dries out.

Corn Fritters

1 cup frozen corn
2 eggs, separated
1 cup skim milk
1 teaspoon baking soda
1 cup all-purpose flour
safflower oil for frying

SERVES 4

Defrost frozen corn and drain. In a large mixing bowl, mash corn with potato masher or pastry cutter. Mix in egg yolks and milk.

Combine baking soda and flour. Stir into corn mixture. In a separate bowl, whip egg whites until stiff, then fold into batter.

Spray frying pan with non-stick oil and lightly coat with safflower oil. Heat pan over medium burner. When oil is hot, drop batter by heaping tablespoon, frying until golden brown on both sides

COASTAL NEW ENGLAND   WINTERFARE COOKING

Refreshed Winter Peas

This simple recipe puts a fresh taste back into frozen peas.

1 lb. frozen peas
2 teaspoons butter
1 tablespoon vegetable
    bouillon
½ cup finely chopped
    onion
1 teaspoon chopped mint
salt and pepper to taste

SERVES 6

Warm peas, just until tender. Drain.

While peas are heating, melt butter and sauté onion until clear. Pour over peas, add mint, salt and pepper. Toss lightly and heat in covered pot 1 minute before serving.

The simple pea is an excellent year-round food. The fresh tender peas of spring are sweet and crunchy right off the vine. Dried peas have provided winter nourishment for thousands of years. Peas can also be preserved by canning, freezing and pickling. They contain protein, carbohydrates, Vitamins A, B complex and C, iron and calcium.

COASTAL NEW ENGLAND   WINTERFARE COOKING

Green Beans Amandine

1 lb. frozen green beans
1 teaspoon butter
2 tablespoons white wine
3 tablespoons sliced
    almonds
pinch of salt
$^1/_2$ teaspoon pepper

SERVES 4

Warm green beans in covered pot until tender, but not limp. Drain and return to pot.

While green beans are cooking, toast sliced almonds on baking sheet in 300° oven, then sauté in butter and wine. Pour over drained green beans. Add salt and pepper, toss to coat. Serve hot.

Gosport Church
Star Island, Isles of Shoals
New Hampshire

Honey-Glazed Turnips

8 small whole turnips
1 teaspoon butter
1 tablespoon safflower oil
2 tablespoons honey
2 teaspoons lemon juice
salt and pepper to taste

SERVES 4

Peel turnips and cut into quarters. Simmer in boiling water 30 minutes, or until tender. Drain, and place in serving bowl.

While turnips are cooking, melt butter with oil in a small saucepan. Add honey, lemon juice, salt and pepper, and warm over low heat. Pour sauce over turnips in serving bowl.

COASTAL NEW ENGLAND   WINTERFARE COOKING

Sherried Mushrooms Au Gratin

1 lb. mushrooms
1 small onion
4 whole cloves
1 small bay leaf
2 tablespoons olive oil
1½ tablespoons flour
1 cup skim milk
pinch of salt
pinch of pepper
pinch of nutmeg
3 tablespoons sherry
2 teaspoons grated
    Parmesan cheese

Optional:
15 shucked oysters

SERVES 5

Cut large mushrooms in quarters and small mushrooms in half. Chop onion and tie in cheesecloth with cloves and bay leaf to make a spice bag.

In a saucepan over low heat, warm olive oil, then blend in flour. With a whisk, stir in milk, salt, pepper and nutmeg until smooth. Place spice bag in sauce. Cook on low heat 15 minutes, stirring frequently. When thickened, remove spice bag, stir in sherry.

Preheat oven to 375°. Spray oven dish with non-stick oil. Place mushrooms, and oysters if desired, in dish. Cover with sauce, then sprinkle with Parmesan. Bake 25 minutes, or until nicely browned on top.

COASTAL NEW ENGLAND   WINTERFARE COOKING

Broccoli Dijonnaise

Dijonnaise is a wonderful sauce that can be poured over most steamed vegetables. This recipe makes 2 cups of Dijonnaise.

1 large head broccoli

SERVES 4

Dijonnaise Sauce:
1 tablespoon canola oil
$1/3$ cup chopped onion
$1/4$ teaspoon thyme
$1/4$ teaspoon garlic powder
$1/2$ bay leaf
1 cup vegetable broth
1 cup canned tomatoes
2 tablespoons canola oil
2 tablespoons flour
1 cup skim milk
$1/4$ teaspoon nutmeg
1 tablespoon Dijon
    mustard
2 tablespoons Madeira

Divide broccoli into large florets. Just before Dijonnaise is ready, steam broccoli about 7 minutes, until it has just turned tender.

Sauté onion in 1 tablespoon oil until clear. Add spices. Mix in broth (can be made from bouillon cube). Chop tomatoes into small pieces, drain and add to broth. Simmer until liquid is reduced by half. Remove bay leaf.

In a separate saucepan, heat 2 tablespoons oil, blend in flour, then whisk in milk and nutmeg. Blend and cook until thick and smooth. Combine both sauces, stir in Dijon mustard, Madeira, salt and pepper to taste.

COASTAL NEW ENGLAND   WINTERFARE COOKING

Curry Creamed Cauliflower and Peas

1 head cooked cauliflower
    ($2^1/_2$ cups florets)
2 cups frozen peas
2 tablespoons canola oil
2 tablespoons wheat flour
2 teaspoons curry
1 teaspoon turmeric
$^1/_2$ teaspoon ground
    cardamom
1 cup skim milk
pinch of salt
1 tablespoon chopped
    parsley
pinch of paprika

SERVES 6

Set cauliflower and peas over low heat to warm. Do not overcook.

Heat oil in a large saucepan. Blend in flour and seasonings to make a roux. Use a whisk to mix in milk. Stir until sauce is smooth and thick. Drain vegetables, add to sauce and heat together. Place in serving bowl, and sprinkle with parsley, salt and paprika.

COASTAL NEW ENGLAND   WINTERFARE COOKING

New Potatoes

1¹/₂ lbs. small red potatoes
1 tablespoon butter
3 tablespoons olive oil
¹/₂ cup scallions, finely chopped
1 teaspoon crushed garlic
2 teaspoons lemon juice
1 teaspoon dill
pinch of salt
pinch of pepper

SERVES 6

Scrub potatoes and place in a large pot of boiling water. Simmer for 20-25 minutes, until potatoes are tender but not mushy.

While potatoes are cooking, melt butter with olive oil. Briefly sauté scallions and garlic, then add lemon juice and spices. Drain potatoes and place in serving bowl. Pour sauce over potatoes, and toss to coat.

Rhode Island calls itself "The Ocean State." By navigating the deep waters of Narragansett Bay, a large ship can sail two-thirds of the way through the state. Providence is at the head of the bay, and Newport on an island at its mouth. In Colonial times, these cities were maritime trade centers for fish, lumber, shipbuilding, rum, and even ponies.

COASTAL NEW ENGLAND   WINTERFARE COOKING

Candied Cranberry Sweet Potatoes

4 medium-sized sweet
   potatoes
1 cup fresh cranberries
$^1/_2$ cup apple juice or cider
$^3/_4$ cup brown sugar
3 tablespoons lemon juice
$^1/_3$ cup honey
1 tablespoon melted
   butter

SERVES 4

Cut sweet potatoes in half and boil in water until tender. Cool in cold water, then peel off skins. Place sweet potatoes in a baking dish that's been sprayed with non-stick oil.

In a saucepan, combine cranberries, apple juice or cider and brown sugar. Cook about 25 minutes. Mix in lemon juice and spoon cranberry sauce over sweet potatoes. Combine honey with melted butter and pour on top. Bake in preheated oven 20 minutes.

The riverboat *Becky Thatcher* on the Connecticut River by the Goodspeed Opera House. Haddam, Connecticut

COASTAL NEW ENGLAND   WINTERFARE COOKING

Grilled Eggplant Italiano

Filling:
1/2 cup grated part-skim
    mozzarella cheese
6 tablespoons grated
    Parmesan cheese
3/4 cup part-skim Ricotta
    cheese
1 egg
1 teaspoon oregano
1 tablespoon parsley
basil and pepper to taste

Batter:
1 egg
3 tablespoons flour
2/3 cup skim milk
1 tablespoon canola oil

2 small eggplants
4 tablespoons canola oil
flour for dipping
2 cups spiced tomato sauce

SERVES 8

Blend together filling ingredients until smooth. Cover and chill.

Beat batter ingredients together until smooth.

Peel eggplant. Cut lengthwise into thin slices. Spray a large griddle with non-stick oil, then coat with canola. Preheat on medium-high. Dip eggplant slices in flour, then in batter. Fry in griddle until lightly browned on both sides. Drain on paper towels.

While eggplant is still warm, spoon 2 tablespoons filling mixture across eggplant, near the wider end. Roll up loosely, jelly-roll style. Place in baking dish that's been sprayed with non-stick oil. Cover with tomato sauce. Bake in preheated 375° oven for 15 minutes.

Spinach-Ricotta Dumplings

SERVES 8

1 lb. frozen, chopped
    spinach
1¹/₂ cups part-skim
    Ricotta cheese
1 cup bread crumbs
2 eggs, beaten
1 clove garlic, minced
1 small onion, chopped
4 tablespoons grated
    Parmesan cheese
1 teaspoon basil
salt and pepper to taste
1 cup wheat or rye flour
2 quarts salt-water

Serve with:
mustard sauce

Rinse and pat dry spinach leaves. Mix spinach with Ricotta, bread crumbs, eggs, garlic, onion, Parmesan, basil, salt and pepper. Roll into 1-inch balls, then roll balls lightly in flour. Chill in refrigerator.

Bring 2 quarts of salt-water to a boil in a deep saucepan. Turn heat to medium-high. Drop spinach-ricotta balls into simmering water. In 4-5 minutes the balls will rise to the surface, indicating they are finished cooking. Remove with a slotted spoon. Serve on toothpicks with your favorite mustard sauce.

COASTAL NEW ENGLAND   WINTERFARE COOKING

Butternut Casserole

6 cups fresh butternut
   squash, peeled and
   cut in ¹/₂-inch pieces
¹/₂ cup chopped onion
1 cup shredded carrots
1 cup chopped celery
2 tablespoons canola oil
1¹/₂ cups bread crumbs
1 teaspoon basil
1 teaspoon thyme
2 cups non-fat plain
   yogurt
¹/₂ cup low-fat Cheddar
1 egg, beaten
¹/₄ cup chopped chives
2 tablespoons toasted
   sesame seeds

SERVES 8

Preheat oven to 350°. Spray a 2-quart casserole with non-stick oil.

Steam squash until tender. Sauté onion, carrots and celery in canola oil. Remove from heat and stir in bread crumbs, basil, thyme, and salt and pepper to taste. Place half of the squash in the casserole, cover with stuffing, and then the other half of the squash.

In a saucepan, combine yogurt and cheese over low heat until cheese melts. Remove from heat and whisk in the beaten egg and chives. Pour over squash, then sprinkle sesame seeds over top. Bake 30 minutes.

Orange Maple Acorn Squash

2 medium-sized acorn
squashes
8 tablespoons maple
syrup
4 tablespoons frozen
orange juice
concentrate
2 teaspoons cinnamon
4 pinches of salt
boiling water

SERVES 4

Preheat oven to 375°. Cut squash lengthwise to show shape. Scoop out seeds and stringy fibers. Place in deep baking dish, open side up, so halves fit snugly into the dish.

Fill center of each squash half with 2 tablespoons maple syrup, 1 tablespoon orange juice concentrate, $1/2$ teaspoon cinnamon and a pinch of salt. Place baking dish on oven rack, then carefully pour 1 inch of boiling water in pan to surround squash. Bake 40 minutes, or until tender and golden brown.

Orange Cranberry Sauce

1 lb. fresh cranberries
1 cup orange juice
$1^1/_2$ cups brown sugar
1 teaspoon cinnamon

Wash cranberries. Cook in orange juice until their skins burst, then cook 5 minutes more. Stir in sugar and cinnamon. Serve warm, or chill to firm and use as a relish.

COASTAL NEW ENGLAND   WINTERFARE COOKING

Sesame Brussels Sprouts

1 lb. Brussels sprouts
1 tablespoon butter
$^1/_2$ cup crushed crumbs
     from rye crackers
2 tablespoons sesame
     seeds
2 tablespoons grated
     Parmesan cheese

Optional:
$^1/_2$ cup roasted and
     chopped chestnuts

SERVES 4

Steam Brussels sprouts until tender. In a small pan, melt butter, toss in crumbs and sesame seeds. Toast until golden.

Drain Brussels sprouts. Combine with cheese, and if desired, chestnuts. Transfer into casserole sprayed with non-stick oil. Sprinkle top with toasted crumbs and sesame seeds. Bake in 350° oven 25 minutes.

By 1860, most American homes had an iron cooking range, instead of a searing open hearth fire. Besides ease of use and overall convenience, precision of heat became a possibility. In 1880 gas was widely available, and these stoves replaced the solid-fuel models. Electric "hot plate" stoves hit the market in 1890, but were not popular until the 1920's.

Braised Leeks

6 leeks
2 tablespoons lemon juice
$^1/_2$ cup vegetable bouillon
2 teaspoons sugar
1 teaspoon white pepper
1 teaspoon butter

SERVES 4

Remove and discard upper leaves and tough outer green stalks from leeks. Wash leeks well, then slice in half lengthwise. Spray stove-top skillet or casserole with non-stick oil. Arrange leeks in skillet.

In a small mixing bowl, combine remaining ingredients, then pour over leeks. Bring to a boil over medium-high heat. Cover and reduce heat to low. Simmer for 25 minutes, or until tender.

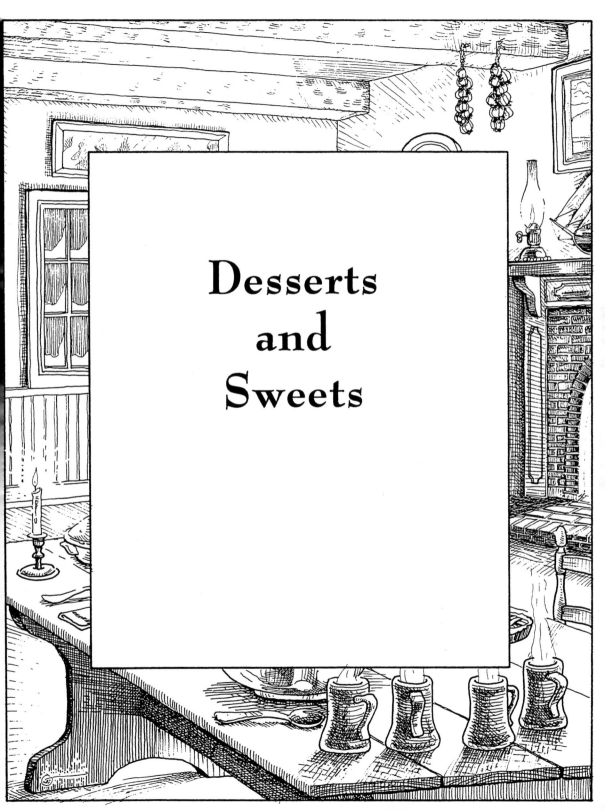

Desserts
and
Sweets

CONTENTS

Cherry Tart

Tart Shells:
1 cup all-purpose flour
2 tablespoons sugar
5 tablespoons canola oil
1 egg yolk
$^1/_2$ teaspoon vanilla
1 tablespoon lemon juice
3 tablespoons
    confectioner's sugar

Cherry Tart Filling:
$^1/_2$ cup apple juice
3 tablespoons quick-
    cooking tapioca
1 tablespoon butter
$^1/_2$ cup sugar (more if
    cherries are bitter)
$^1/_2$ cup brown sugar
1 tablespoon lemon juice
4 cups unsweetened
    canned, frozen or
    fresh pitted cherries

MAKES SIX 3-INCH TARTS

Tart Shells: Combine flour and sugar. Using a pastry cutter or fingertips, work canola oil into flour. Make well in center, add egg yolk, vanilla and lemon juice. Mix with fingers until dough forms a ball and is not sticky. Cover and refrigerate 30 minutes. Roll dough between sheets of wax paper to $^1/_8$-inch thickness. Cut out tarts to line pans. Dough can also be cut to fit tins for large muffins, with sides of tart $1^1/_2$-inches high. Bake in 400° oven 7-9 minutes. Unmold shells, cool on wire rack. Dust with confectioners sugar.

Filling: Mix apple juice and tapioca in a small bowl. Combine butter, sugars and lemon juice in a saucepan. Drain cherries and add to saucepan, cook 10 minutes over medium-low heat. Add tapioca mixture and bring to a boil. Remove from heat. Cool at room temperature 10 minutes before pouring filling into shells.

Holiday Strudel

This strudel has been present (but not for long) at all major family celebrations and holidays since my grandmother wrote it 60 years ago.

Filling:
1 large lemon
2 cups golden raisins
1 cup chopped pecans
1 lb. each unsweetened
    pineapple, peach,
    apricot and orange
    marmalade preserves
$^1/_2$ cup shredded coconut
2 tablespoons quick
    tapioca
$^1/_2$ cup plain bread crumbs

Pastry Dough:
2 cups flour
$^1/_8$ teaspoon baking soda
2 tablespoons sugar
2 eggs
$^1/_4$ cup canola oil
$^1/_2$ teaspoon vinegar
$1^1/_2$ tablespoons water
brushing/tops: canola oil,
    cinnamon, sugar

MAKES 100 PIECES

In a large bowl, squeeze juice from lemon and grate rind. Add remaining filling ingredients. Mix, cover and refrigerate 24 hours.

Combine pastry dough ingredients in a mixer, keep covered to prevent drying out. On a floured cloth, roll a 2-inch ball of dough into a thin 12" x 8" rectangle. Lightly brush with oil. Place $1^1/_2$-inch wide by $^3/_4$-inch high strip of filling along a 12-inch edge. Use the cloth to raise the edge and roll up the strudel. Pinch ends, and transfer to cookie sheet sprayed with non-stick oil. Place rolls 2-inches apart on cookie sheet. Brush with oil, sprinkle with cinnamon and sugar. With a sharp knife (starting $^1/_2$-inch from ends) pierce top of roll at 1-inch intervals. Bake in 350° oven for 25 minutes. Cool on pan 10 minutes, then on brown paper. Cut into pieces at pierced marks, and separate to cool.

COASTAL NEW ENGLAND   WINTERFARE COOKING

Maple Apple Pie

2²/₃ cups all-purpose
   flour
4 tablespoons sugar
1 teaspoon salt
¹/₂ cup canola oil
6 tablespoons cold skim
   milk
6 cups apples, peeled
   and sliced
1 tablespoon lemon juice
¹/₂ cup maple syrup
¹/₂ cup brown sugar
¹/₂ teaspoon vanilla
   extract
2 tablespoons cornstarch
4 tablespoons apple juice
1 tablespoon butter
1 tablespoon sugar
1 teaspoon cinnamon

NOTE: Hot pie is best
after cooling 20 minutes.

MAKES ONE 9-INCH PIE

Sift flour, sugar and salt together. In a separate bowl, combine oil and milk. Pour into flour, then blend with a fork and roll into a ball. If too dry to hold together, add a little milk. Wrap in plastic and chill 15 minutes. Divide dough into 2 pieces. Roll each piece between sheets of wax paper. Place one in pie dish sprayed with non-stick oil. After crust is filled, place the other piece on top, pinch edges together, flute and trim.

Preheat oven to 400°. Mix apples, lemon juice, maple syrup, brown sugar and vanilla. Dissolve cornstarch in apple juice, stir into apples. Rest 15 minutes then stir again. Pour into crust, spread evenly and dot with butter. Place top crust on pie as stated above. Make slits in top crust. Sprinkle with cinnamon and sugar. Bake about 40 minutes.

COASTAL NEW ENGLAND   WINTERFARE COOKING

Persimmon Pumpkin Pie

Here's an interesting recipe for the beautiful persimmon. Early colonists' winter meals frequently included pumpkin and persimmon.

2 cups all-purpose flour
3 tablespoons sugar
6 tablespoons canola oil
4 tablespoons ice water
1 tablespoon skim milk
1 native persimmon
    (non-Japanese variety)
2 cups cooked or canned
    mashed pumpkin
$1^1/_2$ cups skimmed
    evaporated milk
$^1/_3$ cup molasses
$1^1/_2$ cups brown sugar
3 eggs, slightly beaten
1 teaspoon baking powder
2 teaspoons cinnamon
1 teaspoon nutmeg

SERVES 8

Combine flour and sugar in mixing bowl. Using pastry cutter or two knives, cut in oil until consistancy of peas. Add water and milk. Cover with plastic, chill in refrigerator 15 minutes. Spray large pie plate with non-stick oil. Roll dough between layers of waxed paper. Place in pie plate, flute and trim edges. Lightly spray shell with vegetable oil.

Steam whole persimmon 25 minutes, then cool, cut and press through colander. Mix persimmon pulp with remaining ingredients, beat well. Pour into pie shell. Bake in preheated 425° oven for 15 minutes, reduce heat to 350° and bake 35 minutes more.

The North American persimmon was introduced to the early settlers by the Indian women. Though at first thought inedible, the Indians told the newcomers to not harvest the fruit until after the first frost (when the persimmon loses its astringency). Persimmons were then used in preserves, dried, and reduced to flour for breads and puddings.

COASTAL NEW ENGLAND   WINTERFARE COOKING

Cranberry Walnut Ring

2 cups cranberries
1$^1/_2$ cups sugar
1 tablespoon finely
    grated orange rind
2 tablespoons softened
    butter
2 tablespoons safflower
    oil
1 egg
2 cups all-purpose flour
pinch of salt
1 teaspoon nutmeg
1 teaspoon cinnamon
1 cup skim milk
$^1/_2$ cup chopped walnuts

SERVES 10

Preheat oven to 350°. Put cranberries in blender with $^1/_2$-cup sugar and process until coarsely chopped. Transfer cranberries to saucepan and cook 5 minutes over low heat, stirring constantly. Remove from heat and add orange rind

In a medium mixing bowl, cream together butter, oil, remaining cup of sugar and egg. In a separate bowl, sift together flour, salt, nutmeg and cinnamon. Alternately add flour mixture and milk to the cranberry mixture, stirring constantly. Fold in chopped walnuts.

Spray a Bundt pan with non-stick oil. Pour batter into pan and bake 40-45 minutes, or until toothpick inserted in center of cake comes out clean. Remove from oven and cool 10 minutes in pan before turning out onto wire rack to cool.

COASTAL NEW ENGLAND   WINTERFARE COOKING

Pear Compote

4 fresh pears
$1/4$ cup sugar
1 tablespoon finely grated
   lemon zest
1 tablespoon fresh lemon
   juice
$1/4$ teaspoon powdered
   ginger

SERVES 4

Peel, core and cut pears into large pieces. In a large saucepan whisk together sugar, lemon zest, lemon juice and ginger. Add pears.

Cook over medium-low heat 3 minutes, stirring constantly. When pears start to juice-up, raise heat and gently simmer 8 minutes, stirring occasionally.

Serve immediately, or store in refrigerator in covered container.

COASTAL NEW ENGLAND   WINTERFARE COOKING

Boston Cream Pie

Cake Batter:
$^1/_2$ cup safflower oil
$2^1/_2$ cups sifted cake flour
1 tablespoon baking
     powder
$^1/_2$ teaspoon salt
$1^3/_4$ cups sugar
1 cup skim milk
1 teaspoon vanilla extract
2 eggs

Cream Filling:
$^1/_2$ cup sugar
$2^1/_2$ tablespoons
     cornstarch
$1^1/_2$ cups skim milk
2 egg yolks
1 teaspoon vanilla extract

Topping:
confectioner's sugar

SERVES 8

Cakes: Preheat oven to 350°. Spray two 9-inch round layer cake pans with non-stick oil. In a large mixing bowl, use electric beaters to blend cake batter ingredients. Beat 3 minutes on high speed. Pour into baking pans. Bake 30 minutes, or until toothpick inserted in cakes comes out clean. Cool in cake pans for 10 minutes, then turn onto wire rack and cool thoroughly.

Cream Filling: In a saucepan, mix sugar, cornstarch, milk and egg yolks. Stirring constantly, cook over medium heat until mixture boils for one minute. Remove from heat and stir in vanilla. Cool to room temperature before layering.

Spread cream filling between cake layers and sprinkle top of Boston Cream Pie with confectioner's sugar.

COASTAL NEW ENGLAND   WINTERFARE COOKING

Plum Sorbet

2 cups plums, fresh
    frozen, or canned
$^{1}/_{2}$ cup apple juice
$^{1}/_{4}$-$^{1}/_{2}$ cup sugar,
    depending on
    sweetness of plums
lemon wedges

SERVES 4

Blend plums in blender. With a sieve, strain skins from purée.

Combine apple juice with sugar in a saucepan. Stir over low heat until sugar is dissolved. Remove from heat and mix in plum purée.

Pour into 8-inch square pan and place in freezer. Using spatula, stir every 15 minutes until creamy, about 2 hours, then cover and allow to freeze. To serve, scoop into small dishes and garnish with lemon wedges.

In 1845, John Brundy Brown opened the Portland Sugar House utilizing a new process to convert molasses into a high grade of "white" sugar. He produced 250 barrels a day, and grossed over $1,500,000 a year. To supply the Sugar House, Mr. Brown kept a fleet of brigs and schooners sailing from Matanzas and Cardenas to Portland, Maine.

COASTAL NEW ENGLAND   WINTERFARE COOKING

Blueberry Tea Cake with Honey

2 cups all-purpose flour
4 tablespoons cornmeal
2 teaspoons baking
  powder
1 teaspoon baking soda
1/4 cup brown sugar
1 teaspoon nutmeg,
  cinnamon or cloves
2 tablespoons melted
  butter
1 egg
1 cup honey
1 cup low-fat buttermilk
1 teaspoon vanilla extract
3 cups blueberries, tossed
  in 1 tablespoon flour

Glaze:
1 cup confectioner's sugar
1 teaspoon almond
  extract
2+ tablespoons skim milk

SERVES 12

Preheat oven to 350°. Spray 9" x 5" loaf pan, 7" x 11" cake pan, or three 6-ounce metal juice cans with non-stick vegetable oil.

In a large mixing bowl, combine all dry ingredients. In a separate bowl, beat together liquid ingredients until creamy. Whip liquid mixture into dry ingredients. Lightly fold flour-coated blueberries into batter. Pour batter into prepared baking pan or divide equally between metal cans. Bake loaf or cake pan 40-45 minutes, or tea-loafs in metal cans about 30 minutes. Allow to cool 10 minutes in pan or cans before removing.

Combine all ingredients for glaze, using just enough milk to make glaze drizzle over cake. While cake is still warm, drizzle glaze over top and down sides. Best if served while still warm, or within 24 hours of baking.

COASTAL NEW ENGLAND   WINTERFARE COOKING

Chocolate Raspberry Torte

6 eggs, separated
$^7/_8$ cup sugar
$^1/_2$ cup bread crumbs,
    (coarse, not fine)
$^1/_2$ cup unsweetened
    grated chocolate
1 teaspoon vanilla
$^1/_2$ cup chopped almonds
$^1/_2$ teaspoon double-acting
    baking powder
$1^1/_2$ cups raspberry jam
1 cup raspberries, fresh
    or frozen, defrosted
    and drained

SERVES 12

Preheat oven to 325°. Have all ingredients at room temperature. Beat egg yolks until light and lemony color. Gradually beat sugar into yolks. Add one-quarter cup of the chocolate, vanilla, almonds and baking powder.

In a separate bowl, beat egg whites until stiff. Gently fold into batter. Pour batter into ungreased 9-inch spring-form or tube pan, so cake can be removed without much handling. Bake 1 hour, then chill torte in refrigerator.

Carefully slice cake into two layers. Slide thin flat platter between layers to lift off the top layer. Melt raspberry jam in small saucepan over low heat. Spread one-third of the jam on top of bottom cake layer. Sprinkle remaining one-quarter cup chocolate over jam. Place top layer back on cake. Spread remaining jam over top and sides. While jam is still warm, place raspberries on top. Chill before serving.

COASTAL NEW ENGLAND   WINTERFARE COOKING

Gingerbread People

My niece, Amanda, would be truly distraught if "Gingerbread" were an exclusive men's club.

$^1/_4$ cup canola oil
$^1/_2$ cup sugar
$^1/_2$ cup dark molasses
$3^1/_2$ cups all-purpose flour
1 teaspoon baking soda
$^1/_4$ teaspoon cloves
$^1/_2$ teaspoon cinnamon
2 teaspoons ginger
pinch of salt
$^1/_4$ cup water

MAKES EIGHT 5-INCH LONG PEOPLE

Preheat oven to 350°. Spray cookie sheet with non-stick oil.

Using electric beater, blend oil, sugar and molasses. Sift flour, then resift with remaining dry ingredients. Mix flour mixture into wet mixture in three parts, alternating each addition with one-third of the water. Roll dough on a lightly floured surface, about $^1/_4$ inch thick. Cut out gingerbread people with cookie cutter or knife. Set on cookie sheet. Use raisins or candied fruits for features and buttons. Bake until dough springs back when lightly pressed, about 8-10 minutes.

Decorating Gingerbread People: For each icing color, blend together $^1/_4$ cup confectioner's sugar, a few drops of water, and 1-2 drops food coloring into a paste. Apply icing with a small knife. To add detail and texture, use a wooden toothpick. (This recipe can also be used to construct Gingerbread Houses.)

COASTAL NEW ENGLAND   WINTERFARE COOKING

New Hampshire Maple Curls

1 cup maple syrup
$\frac{1}{2}$ cup canola oil
1 cup all-purpose flour
pinch of salt

MAKES THIRTY 3-INCH CURLS

Preheat oven to 350°. Spray cookie sheet with non-stick oil.

Boil maple syrup and oil together for 30 seconds. Remove from heat, stir in flour and salt until well blended.

Drop dough by the tablespoon onto cookie sheet, leaving 3 inches between them. Bake 9-12 minutes, until cookie is the color of maple syrup. Remove pan from oven and let cool 1 minute, then remove cookies one at a time. Place handle of wooden spoon on edge of cookie and roll into a curl around handle.

COASTAL NEW ENGLAND   WINTERFARE COOKING

Berry Cream Custard

1 cup frozen berries
    (strawberries,
    raspberries or
    blueberries)
2 cups skim milk
$^1/_4$ cup honey
pinch of salt
2 beaten eggs
$^1/_2$ teaspoon vanilla
$^1/_2$ cup sugar

SERVES 5

Preheat oven to 300°. Spray 5 individual custard cups with non-stick oil.

Set berries to drain in sieve and reserve juice. In a saucepan on medium heat, blend milk, honey and salt, and scald milk.. Remove from heat, whisk in eggs and vanilla. Pour custard filling into prepared cups. Place cups in deep-dish baking pan, then fill baking pan with $1^1/_2$ inches of very hot (not boiling) water. Bake 50 minutes. Chill custard cups.

Boil reserved berry juice with sugar for 10 minutes. Remove from heat, stir in berries. Spoon berry sauce over cooled custard cups.

Spiced Bread Pudding

$2^1/_2$ cups of cubed stale bread
$^1/_2$ cup raisins, dried apples or other fruit
3 eggs
$^1/_2$ cup sugar
pinch of salt
12 oz. can skimmed evaporated milk
$^1/_2$ cup very hot (but not boiling) water
1 teaspoon cinnamon
1 teaspoon nutmeg
2 teaspoons vanilla extract

SERVES 4

Preheat oven to 350°. Spray 2-quart baking dish with non-stick oil.

Put bread cubes in baking dish and cover with raisins or other dried fruit.

In a mixing bowl, beat together eggs, sugar, salt and milk. Slowly beat in the hot water, cinnamon, nutmeg and vanilla. Pour egg mixture over bread and fruit.

Bake bread pudding until light golden on top, about 45 minutes. Tastes best served warm.

COASTAL NEW ENGLAND   WINTERFARE COOKING

Rum-Ricotta Cheesecake

MAKES 9-INCH CHEESECAKE

Cheesecake Crust:
2 cups sugared graham
    cracker crumbs
2 tablespoons canola oil

Cheesecake Filling:
4 eggs
1 cup sugar
1 teaspoon vanilla extract
2 tablespoons rum
8 oz. softened non-fat
    cream cheese
1$^1/_2$ cups part-skim
    Ricotta cheese, well
    drained in sieve
3 tablespoons chopped
    pecans
1 teaspoon flour

Preheat oven to 375°. Spray 9-inch spring-mold pan with non-stick oil.

Combine crust ingredients in mixing bowl. Press cracker crumb mixture into bottom of pan and 2$^1/_2$ inches up sides. Bake for 3 minutes, then chill.

In a mixing bowl, beat eggs until light and foamy. Gradually add sugar, vanilla and rum. Add cream cheese and Ricotta, blend until smooth. Dust pecans with flour, stir into filling and pour into crust. Bake 35-40 minutes. Chill 6 hours before serving.

Chocolate Sugar Plums

Choose a crisp dry day for working with chocolate, and work in a temperature of about 70°, with no drafts.

MAKES 3 LBS.

1 cup dried apricots,
    finely chopped
1 cup golden raisins
$^1/_2$ cup dried currants
1 cup candied orange or
    lemon peel, cherries,
    and other dried or
    glazed fruits
$^1/_2$ cup walnuts or
    pecans, finely ground
1 teaspoon cinnamon
4 tablespoons honey
3 tablespoons rum,
    brandy or water
1 lb. milk or semisweet
    chocolate squares

NOTE: You can make Plain Sugar Plums by rolling the fruit balls in sugar instead of dipping them in chocolate.

In a large mixing bowl, combine dried and glazed fruits, nuts, cinnamon and honey. Add just enough liquor or water to make the mixture slightly sticky. Roll and compress into $1^1/_2$-inch balls. Set balls on wax paper, where they can adjust to a temperature of 70°.

Boil water in lower pan of double boiler. In the top pan, slowly melt chocolate. When chocolate reaches 100° on a candy thermometer, stir constantly. Heat until chocolate reaches 130°, remove from heat and cool to 88°. Adjust burner so water in bottom pan maintains a temperature of 90°. Return chocolate in top pan to double boiler.

Using candy-dipping fork or small slotted spoon dip sugar plums into chocolate. Set on wire rack (with pan below to catch, melt and reuse drippings.) Just before chocolate hardens, set on wax paper to smooth bottoms.

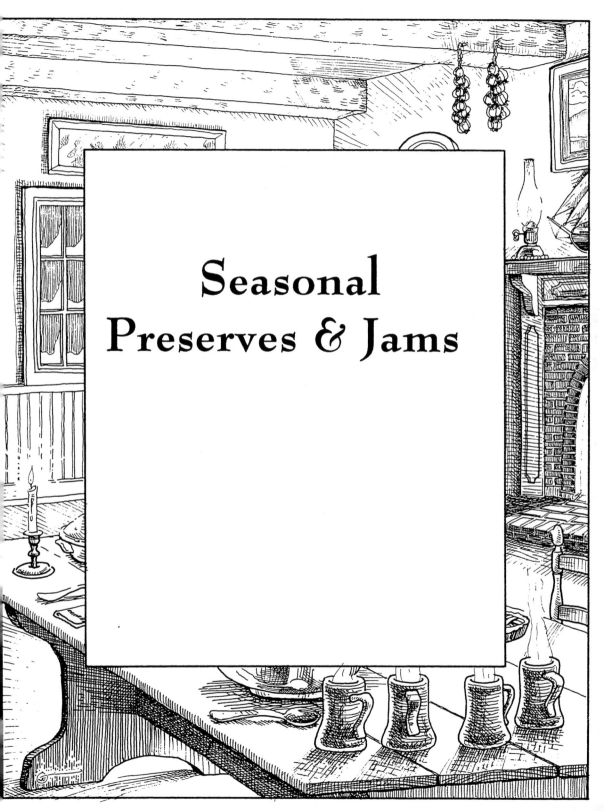

Seasonal Preserves & Jams

CONTENTS

ABOUT CANNING

Jars: Use only properly sealed canning jars with rubber airtight seals or a two-piece metal screw-down lid. Check against defects such as chips or cracks. Jars must be sterilized in boiling water or dishwasher, and filled while still hot.

Packing Jars: Fill while preserves and jar are very hot, leaving $1/4$ to $1/2$-inch headroom. Before sealing, release trapped air by running a butter knife or spatula down the insides of the jar. Wipe top of jar clean before sealing.

Canning at a High Altitude: Increase processing time in boiling water bath by 1 minute for every 1000 feet above sea level.

COASTAL NEW ENGLAND   WINTERFARE COOKING

Citrus Marmalade

1 large grapefruit
3 large oranges
2 lemons
10 cups water
7 cups sugar

MAKES ABOUT 16 JELLY JARS

Scrub fruit well. Halve, and discard seeds.
Scoop pulp into saucepan, then grate in the
rind. Add water and let set for 12 hours.

Boil fruit and water mixture for 20 minutes.
Refrigerate another 12 hours.

Return to stove and warm mixture on low
heat.   Add sugar and stir until dissolved.
Raise heat to moderate, and cook until 222°
is reached on a candy thermometer.

Pour into hot sterilized jars. Seal jars
according to manufacturer's directions.

COASTAL NEW ENGLAND   WINTERFARE COOKING

Currant Jelly

4 lbs. fresh currants, any color or variety

3 cups sugar

MAKES 3 JELLY JARS

Wash currants, but you don't need to trim the stems. Put in a large saucepan, and crush some of the fruit. Cook on low heat for 5 minutes. Raise heat to moderate and cook 25 minutes more.

Strain and squeeze juice through a fine sieve or jelly bag. Return juice to saucepan and add sugar. Stir constantly while sugar dissolves. Continue to cook until temperature reaches 222° on a candy thermometer.

Pour into hot sterilized jars. Seal according to manufacturers directions.

An herbal cough syrup: Pour 1 cup boiling water over 2 tablespoons of dried sweet cicely and steep for 30 minutes. Combine 2 tablespoons of this tea with 2 tablespoons honey and 1 tablespoon lemon juice.

COASTAL NEW ENGLAND   WINTERFARE COOKING

Apple Butter

*For the best flavor, use McIntosh, Jonathan, Golden Delicious
or other good-cooking apple varieties.*

4 lbs. apples
1 cup water
1 cup cider vinegar
$1^1/_2$ cups brown sugar
1 teaspoon cloves
2 teaspoons allspice
1 teaspoon finely grated
    lemon rind
2 teaspoons lemon juice

MAKES 5 PINTS

Clean and quarter apples. Cook slowly in water and vinegar for 35 minutes. Press pulp through a strainer. Discard skin and seeds.

Mix pulp with remaining ingredients. Return to pan and cook over low heat for 25 minutes, stirring constantly to keep from sticking. Apple butter is done when a small amount placed on a plate shows no rim of liquid separating from the butter.

Pour into hot sterilized jars.   Seal jars according to manufacturer's directions.

COASTAL NEW ENGLAND   WINTERFARE COOKING

Winter Fruit Conserve

1 lemon
1 orange
3 pears
3 apples, red or green
2 cups cranberries
1 cup raisins
2 cups honey
$^1/_2$ cup orange juice
2 cups brown sugar
1 tablespoon cinnamon
1 teaspoon ginger
$^1/_2$ cup chopped walnuts

MAKES 8 CUPS

Prepare the fruit as follows and put in a large pot: Cut lemon and orange in half, remove seeds and scoop pulp into pot. Cut unpeeled pears and apples into bite-sized pieces, add to pot with whole cranberries, raisins, honey, orange juice, sugar and spices.

Bring to a boil for 2 minutes. Reduce heat and simmer until temperature reaches 220° on a candy thermometer, about 45 minutes. Add walnuts and pack in hot sterilized jars.

Will keep in refrigerator for 1 week, or seal lid according to manufacturer's directions.

Lemon Curd

My favorite spread on toast, biscuit or waffles.
Contains only 1 gram of fat per teaspoon. Enjoy!

1 cup sugar
3 eggs
2 egg yolks
$^3/_8$ cup lemon juice
1 teaspoon cornstarch
4 tablespoons melted
   butter
4 tablespoons finely
   grated lemon rind

MAKES $1^1/_2$ CUPS

Combine sugar, eggs and egg yolks in a small bowl. Beat with electric beater for 2 minutes, then beat in lemon juice and cornstarch.

Pour mixture into saucepan. Cook over medium heat, stirring constantly, for 10 minutes or until thickened.

Return cooked mixture to bowl and beat briefly. Continue to beat while gradually adding melted butter and grated lemon rind. Place curd into jars and cover with plastic. Chill and store in refrigerator, where curd will firm. Lemon curd will keep a month or two.

Mostarda

This 4-pint recipe makes extra for holiday gift-giving.
The mustard-fruit preserves will keep in the refrigerator about 2 months.

2 cups sugar
4 cups water
6 inches cinnamon sticks
15 whole cloves
1 teaspoon ground mace
15 peppercorns
2 cups dried apricots
6 dried pineapple rings,
    cut in quarters
$1/_4$ cup currants or raisins
1 lb. fresh chestnuts, in
    the shell
4 cans unsweetened pear
    halves
2 tablespoons dry mustard
3 tablespoons water
$1/_2$ cup whole mustard seed

MAKES 4 PINTS

In a large pot over medium-low heat, dissolve sugar in water. Tie cinnamon, cloves, mace and peppercorns in a cheesecloth, then place bag in the syrup. Simmer 15 minutes. Stir in apricots, pineapple quarters, and currants or raisins. Simmer 40 minutes more. Remove spice bag from sauce.

Put a cross in the flat side of the chestnuts and roast in 375° oven for 10 minutes. Peel chestnuts, chop in quarters and add to sauce. Drain and quarter pears, add to sauce. Stir occasionally and cook 10 minutes more.

Mix dry mustard with 3 tablespoons water, add to sauce. In an ungreased skillet, toast mustard seeds over medium heat, stirring until they pop (about 3 minutes). Mix seeds into mostarda. Seal in hot sterilized jars.

COASTAL NEW ENGLAND   WINTERFARE COOKING

Pickled Cauliflower

2 lbs. cauliflower florets
(heads 2-3 inches
round, with about
2 inches of stalk)
1/4 cup pickling salt
3 cups boiling water
1 1/2 cups vinegar
2 cups water
1 teaspoon sugar
1 bay leaf
1 teaspoon mustard seed
8 peppercorns

MAKES 4 PINTS
Read about canning on page 150.

Put salt and cauliflower in boiling water. Simmer 10 minutes, drain. Pack cauliflower in sterilzed jars. Boil remaining ingredients together 5 minutes and pour over cauliflower, leaving 1/2-inch headroom. Seal jars.

Place jars on rack in boiler half-filled with boiling water, with space between jars. Add boiling water to cover jars 2 inches above their tops. Bring to a boil, cover and process 15 minutes. Using tongs, lift jars (not by the lids) and set on towels with several inches between them to cool.

By around 10,000 B.C., in the Near East and Asia, men had specialized their knowledge in the ways of animals, and women in the ways of plants. The historical record indicates these women were the first farmers, who studied and cultivated the natural tendencies of plants and their propagational preferences.

COASTAL NEW ENGLAND   WINTERFARE COOKING

Pepper-Onion Chutney

6 sweet colored peppers,
   chopped fine
6 green peppers,
   chopped fine
6 large onions,
   chopped fine
4 tomatoes, skinned,
   seeded and finely
   chopped
1 quart vinegar
1 tablespoon pickling salt
$^1/_2$ cup honey
1 teaspoon mustard
   powder
1 teaspoon celery seed

MAKES TWO 1-POUND JARS
Read about canning on page 150

Combine all ingredients and bring to a boil. Simmer until somewhat thickened, about 45 minutes. Pack in hot sterilized jars, leaving $^1/_2$-inch headroom in each. Seal jars.

Place jars on rack in boiler half-filled with boiling water, leaving space between them. Add boiling water to cover jars 2 inches above their tops. Bring to a boil, cover, process 15 minutes. Using tongs, lift jars (not by the lids) and set on towels with several inches between them to cool.

COASTAL NEW ENGLAND   WINTERFARE COOKING

Eggnog

2 eggs, separated
2 tablespoons sugar
$^1/_2$ cup skim milk
$^1/_4$ cup non-fat powdered
   milk
$^1/_4$ cup rum, brandy or
   whisky
pinch of ground nutmeg
   (optional)

SERVES 2

Beat egg yolks until light. Slowly beat in sugar, milk, powdered milk and liquor.

In a separate bowl, whip egg whites until stiff. Gently fold egg whites into eggnog mixture and serve in punch glasses.   If desired, sprinkle with nutmeg.

COASTAL NEW ENGLAND   WINTERFARE COOKING

The Coastal New England Cooking Series

Notes on Using these books:

Each book is oriented to take advantage of the fresh produce of the season. Always try to buy locally grown produce, in the freshest condition possible. Your foods will then provide the most flavor and vitamins, and should be the most economical as well.

To allow for a diversity of foods, fruits and vegetables which freeze or dry well are also used in their preferred state of storage.

Non-fat and low-fat dairy products are readily available, and provide calcium, protein, nutrition and flavor, with much less fat. They are incorporated into these recipes and are an excellent substitute to whole milk products.

Fresh produce, fish, grains, flours, dairy and beans provide a diverse and healthy diet, without the animal fats and other problems associated with meat.

Non-stick oil spray is intended to mean a non-fat vegetable oil spray. When used in addition to a cooking oil, it allows the use of less oil.

Preheating the oven or broiler takes only 15 minutes. Save electricity: don't warm your appliances until 15 minutes before they will be used.

COASTAL NEW ENGLAND   WINTERFARE COOKING

Following the Guidelines of
The American Heart Association

A complete and detailed statement of the Guidelines of the American Heart Association can be obtained by contacting your local chapter. This book presents a common-sense approach to following these guidelines without the detailed weighing and measuring of each food item.

By deleting meat and chicken from your diet, a large amount of saturated fat (an artery-damaging fat) will be replaced by more healthful protein and fats. Saturated fats should be limited to 10% of calories. Animal products, including cheese, also contain cholesterol, and their use should be limited.

Polyunsaturated fat (found in salmon, leafy vegetables and seeds) will reduce cholesterol in the blood. Polyunsaturated Omega-3 fatty acids are believed to have an anticlotting agent, and assist in preventing heart attack and stroke.

Monounsaturated fats also reduce the damaging LDL cholesterol, and are found in olive and canola oils.

Total fat intake should not exceed 25-30% of the calories consumed. Even polyunsaturated and monounsaturated fats should be consumed in limited quantities, and will achieve the greatest results if they replace, not supplement, the saturated fats presently consumed.

COASTAL NEW ENGLAND   WINTERFARE COOKING

Following the Guidelines of
The American Heart Association

(cont.) Make a habit of reaching for fruit or naturally sweetened products. The recipes in this book offer a reasonable alternative to the traditional high-fat and caloric desserts, but they are not intended to be eaten everyday, or in volumes greater than those proportionately shown as a serving.

It is critical that the volume of prepared food products be kept to reasonable proportions. In this way, a wide variety of foods can be enjoyed, and you will benefit from a broad range of the natural vitamins, minerals and nutrients in foods. Fresh fruits and vegetables may be eaten regularly, without restriction.

Salt intake should follow the advise of your physician, or be limited to 3 grams per day. Recipes in this book can be made without salt or allow for "salt to taste." The desire for salty foods is acquired, you can become more sensitive to the taste of salt by slowly reducing its volume. Try using sea salt in small amounts, it is more flavorful and contains minerals not present in table salt.

Alcohol consumption should not exceed 1-2 drinks per day.

Carbohydrates should make up at least 50-60% of the diet. This includes vegetables, fruits, grains, flours and beans.

Exercise! It makes your body work better, and you feel better.

COASTAL NEW ENGLAND   WINTERFARE COOKING

Suggested Kitchen Tools, Utensils and Stock Items

Kitchen Tools and Utensils:
Set of whisks in assorted sizes
Slotted spoon and spatula
Blender
Double boiler
Non-stick skillet and frying pans in assorted sizes with lids
Oven casseroles with lids
Non-aluminum pots, pans and containers
Rolling pin
Large stainless steel bowl for mixing bread doughs
Pie pans, regular and deep-dish

Stock Items:
A good variety of spices, fresh fruits and vegetables
Non-stick, non-fat vegetable oil spray
Canola, olive and safflower oils
Skim milk
Non-fat powdered milk (to enrich skim milk)
Low-fat buttermilk
Non-fat plain yogurt, cottage cheese and cream cheese
Low-fat and part-skim cheese products

Measurements

a pinch.............................. $^1/_8$ teaspoon or less
3 teaspoons........................ 1 tablespoon
4 tablespoons...................... $^1/_4$ cup
16 tablespoons..................... 1 cup
2 cups.............................. 1 pint
4 cups.............................. 1 quart
4 quarts............................ 1 gallon
8 quarts............................ 1 peck
16 ounces.......................... 1 pound
8 ounces liquid.................... 1 cup
1 ounce liquid..................... 2 tablespoons

Substitutions

1 tablespoon cornstarch............ 2 T. flour or 2 tsp. quick-cooking tapioca
2 teaspoons arrowroot.............. 1 tablespoon cornstarch
1 teaspoon baking powder.......... $^1/_4$ tsp. baking soda + $^1/_2$ tsp. cream of tartar
$^1/_2$ cup brown sugar.................. 2 T. molasses in $^1/_2$ cup granulated sugar
$^3/_4$ cup cracker crumbs.............. 1 cup bread crumbs
1 tablespoon fresh herbs........... 1 teaspoon dried herbs
1 small clove garlic................. $^1/_8$ teaspoon garlic powder
1 fresh onion...................... 2 T. instant minced onion, rehydrated
1 cup whole milk.................. $^1/_2$ c. skimmed evaporated milk + $^1/_2$ c. water
1 cup buttermilk.................. 1 cup non-fat plain yogurt

Index

COASTAL NEW ENGLAND

WINTERFARE COOKING

Index

COASTAL NEW ENGLAND

WINTERFARE COOKING

If you enjoy this seasonal cookbook, try the others in the Coastal New England Cooking series. Each book has 169 pages of great New England recipes, historical and culinary trivia, and the original artwork of local artists. Our unique and beautiful covers complement the flavor of this wonderful collection. Cookbooks are also a gift that will be used for years.

_____ *Coastal New England Spring Cooking*.........................$11.95

_____ *Coastal New England Summertime Cooking*.................$11.95

_____ *Coastal New England Fall Harvest Cooking*................$11.95

_____ *Coastal New England Winterfare & Holiday Cooking*...$11.95

_____ Total Quantity x $11.95.....................$_____

Maine Residents add 6% sales tax..........$_____

Shipping Charge: $2.00 first book, $_____
plus $1.00 for each additional book

TOTAL $_____

Please enclose check or money order made payable to:

"Coastal New England Publications"
P.O. Box 55
Salisbury Cove, Maine 04672

VISA / M.C # _ _ _ _ - _ _ _ _ - _ _ _ _ - _ _ _ _

Expiration Date:_____   Signature _____

For faster service on VISA / Master Card orders, call (207) 288-8988.

Orders paid by personal check shipped within 3 weeks of receipt,
all other orders shipped in 3 business days.